Number at Key Stage 1

core materials for teaching and assessing number and algebra

Mike Askew, Rob Briscoe,
Sheila Ebbutt, Lynda Maple
and Fran Mosley

ISBN 1 874099 30 8
Designed and typeset by Bookcraft, 9 Lower Street, Stroud GL5 2HT
Printed by Five Castles Press, Duke Street, Ipswich, IP3 0AG

Tower Hamlets

KING'S
College
LONDON
Founded 1829

ISLINGTON COUNCIL

Contents

Introduction

The need for this book

This book offers a set of core activities around which to base your scheme of work for number. We have not intended to provide an entire number curriculum at key stage 1 — you will need to supplement our suggestions with your own favourites, practice material, pages from published material, and so on. But we have tried to offer one set of activities for each important strand of number at this level.

This book grew out of the work done by a group of teachers who were attending a course at King's College, London on developing a scheme of work for number. The teachers who produced the original scheme had something that they could use in school. But when this scheme was trialled with other teachers it became apparent that they found it difficult to implement — they had not been through the process of developing the scheme for themselves and so did not 'own' it in any way. A further period of trialling, reshaping and rewriting was necessary.

Thinking about what had happened, it occurred to us that all over the country teachers with responsibility for mathematics were working on schemes of work for their schools. While it is important that teachers and schools are active in developing a scheme they feel comfortable with, it also seems unnecessary for everyone to have to keep reinventing the wheel. Hence this publication, which provides core activities, tried and tested and rewritten as needed, for schools to use as a basis around which to build a scheme they can truly own.

The contents of the book

'Pupils should be given opportunities to: develop flexible methods of working, mentally and orally; use a variety of practical resources and contexts; use calculators both as a means to explore number and as a tool for calculating with realistic data; record in a variety of ways.'
Programme of Study for Number at Key Stage 1

The book contains ten sections, broadly corresponding to the programmes of study for number at key stage 1. It is important that children work in a variety of ways, using a variety of tools, and for this reason each section contains activities using the same five tools: mental methods; number lines, cards and grids; calculators; objects such as base ten blocks or counters; pencil and paper. So, for instance, in the section on Counting there are five activities which use the range of tools described above. This means that in planning a teaching session you have a choice of activities and can choose which tool you prefer to use at that moment — linking cubes because they are familiar, calculators because they aren't familiar, number lines because you want to introduce children to number lines and this is a good way to do it . . .

Another important feature of these activities is that they are designed to be adapted for children working at different levels of attainment. Nearly all the activities can be used with children who are working towards level 1 right through to those working within level 3. The grid at the beginning of each section shows the names of the five activities in that section and indicates what attainment levels they are suitable for.

The five tools

There is no one best way of teaching mathematics. Children respond differently to experiences, and what works for one may not work for another. In order to help children become confident in number they need a broad and balanced curriculum within mathematics itself. They need access to mathematical ideas through a variety of experiences without any particular way of working being dominant. To help achieve this breadth and balance we suggest that children are offered five sorts of experience to embody mathematics.

● *Mental mathematics*

Learning mathematics is ultimately a mental activity. No amount of practical work will help children learn unless they abstract the mental mathematics from the experience. This process of abstraction is far from easy, but if from an early age children are expected to reflect on how they worked something out, to picture things in their heads and to manipulate mental objects, this helps them enormously in the process of abstraction. Teachers are sometimes sceptical that very young children can work in this way. Indeed when you first ask 'what was in your head?' young children often respond with 'nothing'. However, such responses are less a result of children's inability to reflect on their own thinking processes than of their not knowing what would be an acceptable answer. You can help children begin to articulate their mental processes by providing model explanations — both when you explain your own methods and when more experienced children explain theirs.

● *Lines, cards and grids*

Becoming confident with number involves having a sense of the magnitude of numbers, and having a repertoire of symbolic images to draw upon. Number grids of various types (hundred squares, multiplication and addition squares and so on), number lines, and number cards provide rich sources of activity and also offer children a range of mental images that can support the development of mental strategies. Number lines in particular provide a valuable image of numbers which many adults draw on in everyday mental calculation and estimation.

● *Calculators*

There is now a body of research evidence demonstrating that use of calculators does not lead to any lowering of standards. Instead, free access to calculators at all stages of schooling can actually lead to improved attainment within the framework of well-planned mathematics teaching. The calculator activities in this book challenge children, encouraging them to predict 'what will happen next' and asking them to work out how the calculator is operating on numbers.

Working with a calculator, repeatedly adding two.

● *Objects*

It is very important that children continue to do some work with practical materials throughout their primary school career, in order to build sound mental models of mathematical relationships. Each section in the book contains one activity using readily available objects. Sometimes these are 'structured' materials — commercially produced material that embodies a particular mathematical idea. Sometimes they are objects that are simply fun to work with and to count — bottle tops, conkers, cubes or beans.

● *Pencil and paper*

The great advantage of pencil and paper is that it extends our 'mental screens'. Holding several ideas in the head at once is difficult; pencil and paper helps children hold onto ideas by recording them, then play with, sort or manipulate them. Paper and pencil methods are not appropriate as ends in themselves, but are useful as means to an end.

Working with dominoes, finding all the ones whose dots total five.

The importance of discussion

Learning mathematics is essentially a social process and comes about through the sharing of ideas. Discussion is therefore central to all the activities in this book: discussion between you and the children, and discussion between the children themselves. In order to make sure that your time spent with children is fairly shared out you could timetable yourself to be with each group in turn for a discussion session.

Talking is also a way of lessening the demands on your time. For instance, you can:
• talk through activities with the whole class — children who are not going to do an activity immediately will need less instruction when their turn does come
• get children who have already done an activity to explain it to others
• use reporting-back sessions at the end of lessons to set up further work

Teaching and assessing

While children are involved in learning from the activities in this book you can also assess their levels of attainment. Each activity has a section of questions under the heading 'Can the children . . .'. These questions are graded into four levels, pre-level 1, level 1, level 2 and level 3, and can be used to help you judge what a child can and cannot do, and what they do or do not understand. When planning how to use an activity with a group of children you will inevitably 'differentiate by task', choosing a level of difficulty that you feel will suit that particular group. As you see how the children respond you can then 'differentiate by outcome', adapting or extending the activity while the children are still engaged, or noting things to try on another occasion. The activities are sufficiently open in their design to allow for different development to suit different levels of attainment.

$$70 - 35 = 45 \quad 35$$
$$35 - 15 = 20 \quad 20$$
$$35 - 9 = 24 \quad 26$$

The two pieces of work on this page were produced by children working on Approximate Answers (page 86). In this activity the teacher invents 'sums' and asks the children to produce approximate answers — accurate answers are not needed. They then check the answers using a calculator and write them in.

The child who did the piece of work above clearly knows the rough size of the answers — in one case she apparently knew the exact answer. It would be worth discussing with her what strategies she used — 'How did you do that one?' It would also be important to ask some more challenging questions in order to give her an opportunity to show what else she can do.

$$89 + 11 = 99$$
$$= 100$$
$$100 + 1000 = 11000$$
$$1100$$
$$199 + 999 = 199 \quad 1198$$
$$49 + 34 = 71$$
$$= 83$$
$$78 + 99 = 178$$
$$1009 \quad \overline{177}$$
$$+ 11,000$$

The child who did this work has a good idea of the size an answer should be when adding two-digit numbers but his limited understanding of place value notation is holding him back when working with higher numbers.

It would be a good idea to do some work with him on writing numbers over 100 and then come back to this activity to find out what else he can do.

USING THE ACTIVITY PAGES

Children will experience

This section outlines what the pupils might be learning through the experience and hence indicates the main focus of assessment.

Getting started

This section provides an outline of an activity which can be adapted to several different levels of difficulty. It is a good idea to read this section in conjunction with the 'Can the children . . .' boxes. The suggestions in these boxes offer a guide to what children working at different levels can be expected to achieve in this area, and can help you both to initiate and to continue the activity at appropriate levels.

Section of book

We wanted to make clear the way in which this book corresponds with the sub-division of number and algebra in the national curriculum. To do this, we have divided the activities in the book into nine parts. These nine parts are grouped in three sections: Developing an Understanding of Place Value; Number Relationships and Computation; and Solving Numerical Problems. At the foot of every activity page (left and right) is a reminder of which of these three sections this activity is in.

The name of the activity

The name of the activity is at the top of the left-hand page.

Equipment

This section lists what materials you will need to have available.

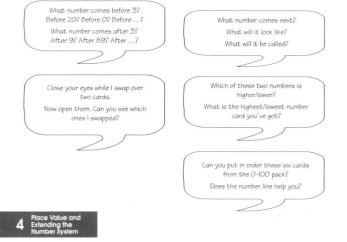

Questions to ask the children

These questions can help focus the children's attention on the mathematics and offer you valuable opportunities for assessment.

Nine parts, five tools

The activities in the book are divided into nine parts. At the top of the right-hand page there is a reminder of which of these nine parts this activity belongs in. Next comes which of the five tools the activity primarily focuses on (for an explanation of the 'five tools' see the Introduction).

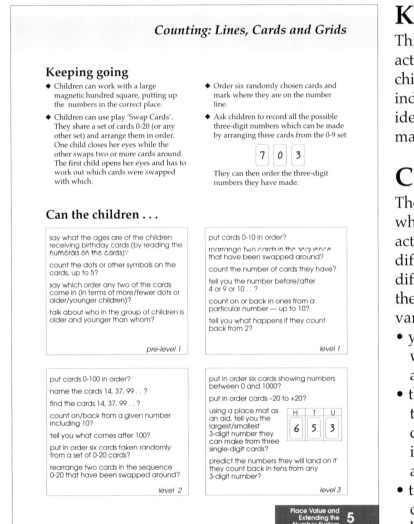

Counting: Lines, Cards and Grids

Keeping going

◆ Children can work with a large magnetic hundred square, putting up the numbers in the correct place.

◆ Children can use play 'Swap Cards'. They share a set of cards 0-20 (or any other set) and arrange them in order. One child closes her eyes while the other swaps two or more cards around. The first child opens her eyes and has to work out which cards were swapped with which.

◆ Order six randomly chosen cards and mark where they are on the number line.

◆ Ask children to record all the possible three-digit numbers which can be made by arranging three cards from the 0-9 set

7　0　3

They can then order the three-digit numbers they have made.

Can the children . . .

say what the ages are of the children receiving birthday cards (by reading the numerals on the cards)?

count the dots or other symbols on the cards, up to 5?

say which order any two of the cards come in (in terms of more/fewer dots or older/younger children)?

talk about who in the group of children is older and younger than whom?

pre-level 1

put cards 0-10 in order?

rearrange two cards in the sequence that have been swapped around?

count the number of cards they have?

tell you the number before/after 4 or 9 or 10 . . ?

count on or back in ones from a particular number — up to 10?

tell you what happens if they count back from 2?

level 1

put cards 0-100 in order?

name the cards 14, 37, 99 . . ?

find the cards 14, 37, 99 . . ?

count on/back from a given number including 10?

tell you what comes after 100?

put in order six cards taken randomly from a set of 0-20 cards?

rearrange two cards in the sequence 0-20 that have been swapped around?

level 2

put in order six cards showing numbers between 0 and 1000?

put in order cards –20 to +20?

using a place mat as an aid, tell you the largest/smallest 3-digit number they can make from three single-digit cards?

H	T	U
6	5	3

predict the numbers they will land on if they count back in tens from any 3-digit number?

level 3

Place Value and Extending the Number System　5

Keeping going

This section offers ways in which the activity can be developed so that the children can continue to work independently, consolidate their ideas, and meet the same mathematics in a different context.

Can the children . . .

These four boxes indicate ways in which the level of difficulty of the activity can be altered by using different equipment or posing different questions. The ideas in these boxes can be helpful in a variety of ways:

• you can use them in deciding at what level of difficulty to start the activity

• they can suggest ways to adjust the level of activity once the children have begun working on it, to meet their different levels of attainment

• they can be used to challenge children to begin to work at a higher level of attainment

• they offer key questions to use in assessing the level of attainment at which individual children are working

Place Value and Extending the Number System

Counting

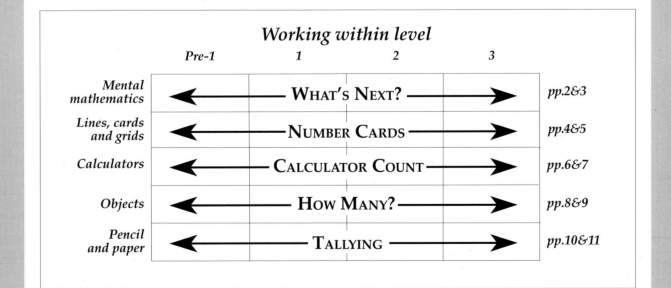

	Working within level				
	Pre-1	*1*	*2*	*3*	
Mental mathematics	←	WHAT'S NEXT?		→	*pp.2&3*
Lines, cards and grids	←	NUMBER CARDS		→	*pp.4&5*
Calculators	←	CALCULATOR COUNT		→	*pp.6&7*
Objects	←	HOW MANY?		→	*pp.8&9*
Pencil and paper	←	TALLYING		→	*pp.10&11*

1

WHAT'S NEXT?

Children will experience

◆ counting on and back in ones

◆ counting on and back past 'difficult' points such as 99, 100, 101 or 21, 20, 19

◆ counting on and back in twos, fives or tens from 0

◆ counting on and back in twos, fives or tens from numbers other than 0

Equipment

◆ number lines or squares for checking

Getting started

In groups, or with the whole class, ask the children to count on or back from certain numbers. (Some children may not understand 'count on' and 'count back', and may prefer 'count up' , 'count down' or some such wording.)

Children can choose what numbers to start from, and how to count (in ones, twos, backwards . . .).

Questions to ask the children

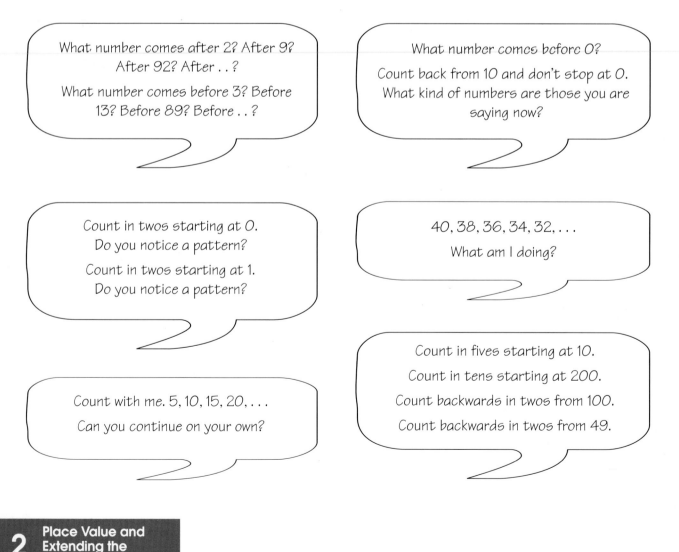

What number comes after 2? After 9? After 92? After . . ?

What number comes before 3? Before 13? Before 89? Before . . ?

What number comes before 0?
Count back from 10 and don't stop at 0. What kind of numbers are those you are saying now?

Count in twos starting at 0. Do you notice a pattern?

Count in twos starting at 1. Do you notice a pattern?

40, 38, 36, 34, 32, . . .
What am I doing?

Count with me. 5, 10, 15, 20, . . .
Can you continue on your own?

Count in fives starting at 10.
Count in tens starting at 200.
Count backwards in twos from 100.
Count backwards in twos from 49.

Keeping going

◆ Children can count as you clap or tap on a drum/tambourine/tin lid.

◆ Children can count as you point to each number on a number line or grid.

◆ Ask children to count as they enter the hall for P.E. then say the same number sequence backwards as they leave.

◆ Teach children to play *Hopscotch* in the playground.

◆ Show children the computer program 'Counter' on *Slimwam 2*.

Can the children . . .

count in order from 1 to their age?

say the next number in the sequence, up to 5?

count down from 5 for a rocket launch?

count in time with clicking fingers or clapping hands?

pre-level 1

---

start at 0 and count on in ones to 10?

start at any number below 10 and count on in ones to 10?

start at 10 and count back in ones to 0?

start at any number below 10 and count back in ones to 0?

level 1

---

start at 0 or any other number and count on in ones to 100?

start at 100, or a smaller number, and count back in ones towards 0?

start at 0 or any other number and count on in twos to 100?

count back in ones and twos from 100?

count past the tens-numbers?
for example — 39, 40, 41 . . .

count on in fives or tens from 0 to 100?

level 2

---

start at 0 or any other number and count on in ones towards 1000?

count past the hundreds-numbers?
for example — 199, 200, 201 . . .

start at any number and count on in twos/fives/tens towards 1000?

count back in ones/twos/fives/tens from 100 towards 0?

count back in ones/twos/fives/tens from any number under 100 towards 0?

count backwards below 0, into negative numbers?

level 3

Number Cards

Children will experience
- counting dots or other objects
- reading numbers
- ordering numbers
- talking about negative numbers

Equipment
- birthday cards showing ages from 1 to 5
- cards showing arrays of dots (or hearts, triangles, ladybirds . . .), from 1 to 10
- number cards 0-100
- number cards −20 to +20
- a set of cards showing random numbers between 0 and 1000
- a number line or grid for checking

Getting started

Ask pairs of children to put a set of cards in order. (Some children may prefer the wording 'put them in line' or 'arrange them like they are on the number line'.)

Children can work with a complete sequence (such as 0-9, 0-100, −20 to +20 or 50-100) or with a random set of cards (such as 9, 12, 25, 45, 55, 61, 69, 82 and 87).

If working with a large set, such as 0-100, make sure children have a good, large space such as the hall floor.

Questions to ask the children

> What number comes before 3? Before 20? Before 0? Before . . ?
>
> What number comes after 3? After 9? After 89? After . . ?

> What number comes next?
>
> What will it look like?
>
> What will it be called?

> Close your eyes while I swap over two cards.
>
> Now open them. Can you see which ones I swapped?

> Which of these two numbers is higher/lower?
>
> What is the highest/lowest number card you've got?

> Can you put in order these six cards from the 0-100 pack?
>
> Does the number line help you?

Keeping going

◆ Children can work with a large magnetic hundred square, putting up the numbers in the correct place.

◆ Two children can play *Swap Cards*. They share a set of cards 0-20 (or any other set) and arrange them in order. One child closes her eyes while the other swaps two or more cards around. The first child opens her eyes and has to work out which cards were swapped with which.

◆ Ask children to order six randomly chosen cards and mark where they are on the number line.

◆ Ask children to record all the possible three-digit numbers which can be made by arranging three cards from the 0-9 set

They can then order the three-digit numbers they have made.

Can the children . . .

say what the ages are of the children receiving birthday cards (by reading the numerals on the cards)?

count the dots or other symbols on the cards, up to 5?

say which order any two of the cards come in (in terms of more/fewer dots or older/younger children)?

talk about who in the group of children is older and younger than whom?

pre-level 1

put cards 0-10 in order?

rearrange two cards in the sequence that have been swapped around?

count the number of cards they have?

tell you the number before/after 4 or 9 or 10 . . ?

count on or back in ones from a particular number — up to 10?

tell you what happens if they count back from 2?

level 1

put cards 0-100 in order?

name the cards 14, 37, 99 . . ?

find the cards 14, 37, 99 . . ?

count on/back from a given number including 10?

tell you what comes after 100?

put in order six cards taken randomly from a set of 0-20 cards?

rearrange two cards in the sequence 0-20 that have been swapped around?

level 2

put in order six cards showing numbers between 0 and 1000?

put in order cards –20 to +20?

using a place mat as an aid, tell you the largest/smallest 3-digit number they can make from three single-digit cards?

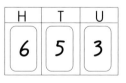

predict the numbers they will land on if they count back in tens from any 3-digit number?

level 3

CALCULATOR COUNT

Children will experience

◆ counting forwards and backwards in ones, twos, and other numbers
◆ the use of the calculator's constant function
◆ recording
◆ predicting and checking predictions

Equipment

◆ desk-top or overhead-projector calculator
◆ calculators with a constant function
◆ numbered and unnumbered number lines
◆ 100-squares

Getting started

Working with a small group, set up a calculator to count on in ones from 0, 20, 100 or another number. (Although calculators vary, with many you can do this by simply pressing ⊞ ① ⊟ .) It is important that all the children can see or hear. Ask them to predict what the next number will be each time, and which digits in the calculator display will change.

You can also get the calculator to count backwards, and to count using negative numbers.

After a while the children can start working on their own counting, starting wherever they please. They may want to write down each guess (perhaps on an unnumbered line) and then the actual number.

Questions to ask the children

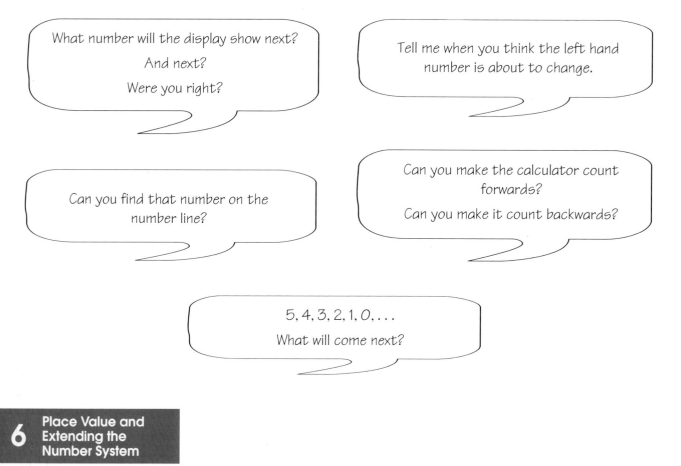

What number will the display show next?
And next?
Were you right?

Tell me when you think the left hand number is about to change.

Can you find that number on the number line?

Can you make the calculator count forwards?
Can you make it count backwards?

5, 4, 3, 2, 1, 0, . . .
What will come next?

Keeping going

◆ Children can start at 0, –10, 20, 30 or 100 on the calculator and write that number on an unnumbered line or grid. They then add or subtract 1 repeatedly, writing in the new number on the line or grid each time.

◆ One child can add 1 repeatedly on the calculator while their partner models the operation by adding to a collection of base ten blocks.

Can the children . . .

read numbers on the calculator display between 1 and 5?

count with you and predict the next number, up to 5?

pre-level 1

predict the next number when you are counting forwards, up to at least ten?

count back along with the calculator, from at least 10 to 0?

level 1

say what will come after 75 when counting forwards? After 89? After 69?

say what will come next after 90 when counting backwards? After 20?

tell you what will happen if they count back past 0?

level 2

predict what will come next after 185 when counting forwards? After 599? After 979?

level 3

HOW MANY?

Children will experience

- matching one to one
- counting (sometimes large numbers of) objects
- structuring their counting

Equipment

- objects to count: counters, cubes, conkers, shells, paper clips, pegs . . .
- containers such as yoghurt pots or bun tins to help children structure their counting
- pegboards
- number lines (0-10, 0-30, 0-100, and 0-1000 numbered in tens)
- number grids and squares

Getting started

You may want to work with the whole class or just with a group.

Show the children a quantity of objects and ask them to count them. (For each level, give children slightly more than you think they can comfortably count.) At first, you may want to count with the children.

If the objects are small or likely to roll off the table, place them on a tray before giving them to the children.

Questions to ask the children

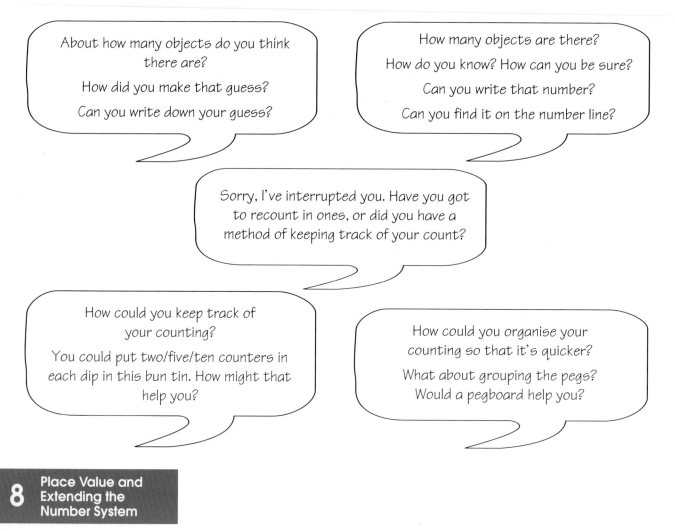

About how many objects do you think there are?

How did you make that guess?

Can you write down your guess?

How many objects are there?

How do you know? How can you be sure?

Can you write that number?

Can you find it on the number line?

Sorry, I've interrupted you. Have you got to recount in ones, or did you have a method of keeping track of your count?

How could you keep track of your counting?

You could put two/five/ten counters in each dip in this bun tin. How might that help you?

How could you organise your counting so that it's quicker?

What about grouping the pegs? Would a pegboard help you?

Keeping going

◆ Keep coming back to counting over a period of time. Children could count linking cubes (good for grouping in twos or tens), seeds in a sunflower, children in class, or lentils in a spoon.

◆ Children can set each other 'guess challenges' — one child puts a certain number of cubes (or other objects) in a jar and makes a secret record of the number. The other children in the class are then encouraged to look at the jar of objects and guess the number.

◆ The children could see how many small things they can put in a matchbox / film canister. They can either collect different things (no two the same), or cram in as many as possible of the same object. If children do the latter, then encourage them each to choose a different object to use. Then they can count and compare, discovering whether more paper clips or paper fasteners or pegs fit in a matchbox.

Can the children . . .

say the numbers up to 5 in order?

match a number word to an object, one to one?

count every object without missing one?

count every object only once?

pre-level 1

organise their counting by moving each object to show they have counted it?

identify the last number as the number of objects in the count — up to 10?

recognise that the total of objects is just one number (that is, if one child says there are 7 and another says it's 5, both cannot be true)?

make a sensible estimate of how many objects they have to count — up to 10?

accept that there are the same number of objects even if they are pushed together, or spread out?

level 1

organise the counting of their objects by grouping them in some way?

keep track of their count if distracted by, for example, recording as they go?

say the numbers in order accurately up to 100, especially when proceeding to the next tens number (for example, 29, 30 . . .)?

make a sensible estimate of how many objects they have to count — up to 100?

level 2

organise the counting of their objects by grouping them in twos, fives, tens, or another grouping?

work systematically in the organisation of their counting?

make a sensible estimate of how many objects they have to count, even over 100?

say the numbers around the tens and hundreds (for example, '109, 110, 111 . . .' or '699, 700, 701 . . .')

level 3

TALLYING

Children will experience
◆ counting objects or events
◆ recording in a structured way
◆ 'reading' a number from a tally record

Equipment
◆ pencil and paper

Getting started

Ask children to keep a tally for five minutes of how many times children in the class stand up (or how many people pass the classroom door / enter the room / leave the room / sharpen a pencil . . .). Children may need to be taught how to tally.

Children who are not able to count in fives may prefer to make a 'two-tally' consisting of crossed strokes — or even single strokes.

Questions to ask the children

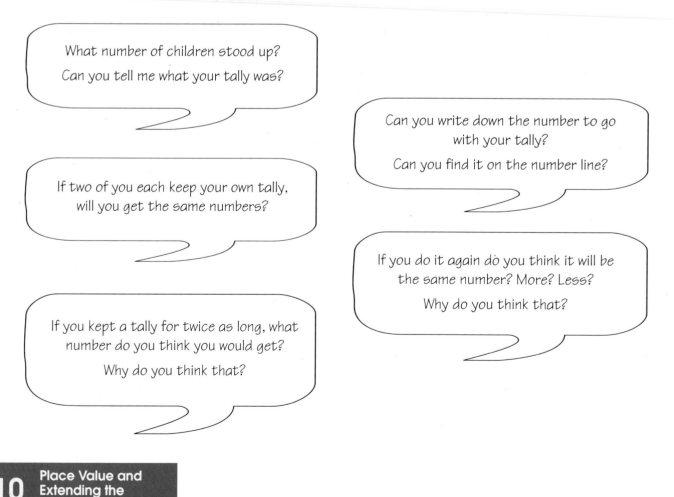

What number of children stood up?
Can you tell me what your tally was?

Can you write down the number to go with your tally?
Can you find it on the number line?

If two of you each keep your own tally, will you get the same numbers?

If you do it again do you think it will be the same number? More? Less?
Why do you think that?

If you kept a tally for twice as long, what number do you think you would get?
Why do you think that?

Keeping going

◆ Children can work in pairs, one watching the time and the other tallying — this would save you effort, and give children the opportunity to read clock and watch dials.

◆ Children could use stones, conkers or beads to tally with, dropping one into a bag for each event. Discuss with them whether they find this easier or harder than keeping a written tally.

◆ The children could make a tally of: children drinking from the fountain at playtime, people passing the classroom door, birds flying past the window, pieces of litter collected from the floor...

◆ Children could have a tally rota so that everyone has a turn tallying. If everyone does five minutes, will their numbers be roughly the same? Why or why not?

Can the children . . .

count people accurately (without tallying) up to 5?

match one pen stroke to one person?

pre-level 1

---

keep an accurate tally of people up to at least 10, using single pen strokes or a two-tally?

'read' the total number represented by their tally record — up to at least 10?

write the total number represented by their tally record — up to at least 10?

level 1

---

keep an accurate tally of people, things or events up to 100, using a five-tally?

'read' the total number represented by their tally record — up to 100?

write the total number represented by their tally record — up to 100?

level 2

---

keep an accurate tally of people, things or events over 100?

'read' the total number represented by their tally record — over 100?

write the total number represented by their tally record — over 100?

level 3

Reading, Writing and Ordering Numbers

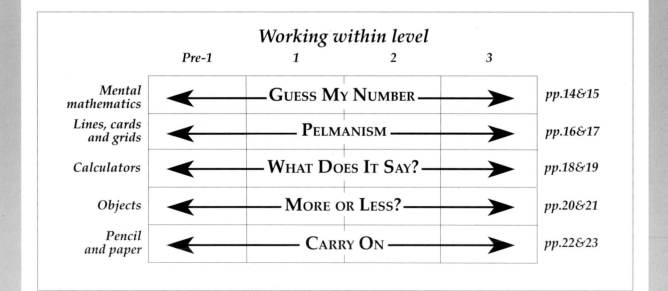

GUESS MY NUMBER

Children will experience

- thinking about the order of numbers in the number sequence
- thinking about the properties of numbers

Equipment

- large sheets of paper and thick felt pens
- 0-30 or 0-100 number cards
- 0-30 or 0-100 number lines
- 100-squares
- objects to count, such as bottle tops or cubes

Getting Started

Do this activity in groups, or with the whole class. Pick a number card and hide it in your pocket. Give them a clue — for example, 'I'm thinking of a number between 0 and 10' — and ask them to find out what the number is. Discourage the children from guessing numbers at random, and encourage them to develop useful questions to give them more clues each time.

With younger children you may wish to have the objects displayed, and then hide them under a cloth.

Once children are familiar with the activity they can take turns to choose a number for the others to guess.

Questions to ask the children

Can you guess my number?

How many guesses did it take to find my number? Can you use fewer questions this time?

Now it's your turn to think of a number and I'll guess.

Is it over 10?

Is it odd?

Does it have a 1 in it?

What information do you now have?

What do you know about the number?

What would be a good question to ask now?

Can you ring on the number line (or square) the numbers that it might be?

Or you could cross out the numbers you have eliminated.

What sort of questions give you the most information?

How can you record your information?

Keeping going

◆ Children take turns to think of a secret number and challenge others to guess — only ten (or twenty) questions allowed.

◆ Children could record their questions and order them according to the amount of information they provide.

◆ Children decide on their own secret number, then write down a series of facts about it which identify it and it alone.

> My Secret Number
> It is odd
> Under 20
> Between 15 and 18

Can the children . . .

make reasonable guesses about small numbers of objects shown to them and then hidden?

show they understand the words 'more' and 'less'?

pre-level 1

ask questions to help them find numbers between 0 and at least 10?

describe numbers between 0 and at least 10 without naming the number?

identify a number that is more/less than 15, 7, 19 . . ?

level 1

ask questions to help them find numbers between 0 and at least 100?

describe numbers between 0 and at least 100 without naming the number?

give and use information such as 'it's odd' or 'it's a multiple of ten' to help identify a number?

level 2

ask questions to help them find numbers between 0 and at least 1000?

discuss which strategies are the most efficient for finding a number?

describe numbers between 0 and at least 1000 without naming the number?

give and use information such as 'it's odd and over 50' or 'it's a multiple of five' to identify a number?

level 3

PELMANISM

Children will experience

◆ recognising and reading numbers using a range of symbols, including digits, words, pictures, and measures. For example, 142, £1.42, 1.42m, 'one hundred and forty two'.

Equipment

◆ birthday cards showing ages of children up to 10 — at least two of each number (for younger children)

◆ about thirty cards showing numbers 0-10 as digits, numbers of dots and pictures (of, for example, six hats) — at least two of each number (level 1)

◆ about fifty cards with numbers up to 100, shown as digits, lines or dots (arranged in arrays of ten) and words — at least two of each number (level 2)

◆ as above but including halves and quarters and some measures (for example, £3.42) (level 3)

Getting started

In pairs or small groups the children turn all the cards face down, and spread them out. The children take it in turns to turn over two cards. If the two cards are equivalent, they keep the pair. If not, the cards are placed face down again.

Younger children could do this activity with the cards face upwards, at least until they are familiar with the cards. They could also play *Snap* and, if you structure the pack so that it consists of 'families' of three or four, *Happy Families*.

Questions to ask the children

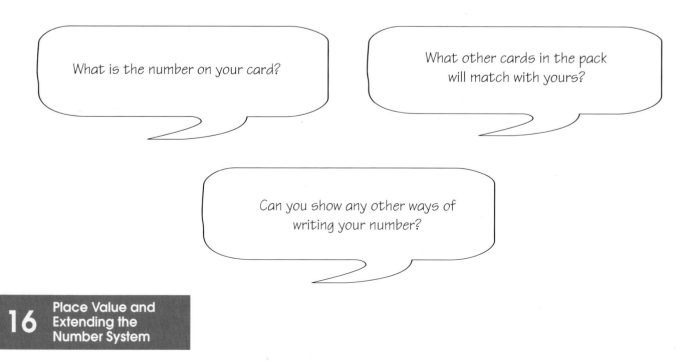

What is the number on your card?

What other cards in the pack will match with yours?

Can you show any other ways of writing your number?

Keeping going

◆ Children could collect examples of numbers written in different ways — perhaps in a scrapbook. (They could include numerals produced by different fonts on a word processor.)

◆ Children could make their own sets of cards, perhaps including Roman or other number scripts.

◆ Go on a number walk and ask the children to draw or photograph numbers they see.

◆ Make a class collection of numbers (including measures) from packages and newspapers.

◆ A group of children can collect stamps or foreign currency and sort them according to the numbers they show.

Can the children . . .

sort the birthday cards according to the numbers on the cards?

talk about the numbers represented, and tell you what they know about them?

pre-level 1

show you picture or dots cards that match with card number 5 (or any other numbers to at least 10)?

say the names of the numbers to at least 10?

on cards showing numbers above 10 identify a number that they are familiar with, such as their door number, a familiar bus number . . ?

level 1

show you dots cards that match with number cards 36, 44, 11 (or any other numbers to at least 100)?

say the names of the numbers to at least 100?

read the spelt-out or numeral form of numbers to at least 100?

tell you which cards they could match with, for example, 'three tens and six units'?

level 2

say the names of the numbers to at least 1000?

read the spelt-out or numeral form of numbers to at least 1000?

find cards to match a card showing, for example, $36^1/_4$?

find cards to match a card showing, for example, 36.25m?

level 3

WHAT DOES IT SAY?

Children will experience
◆ putting numbers in a calculator display
◆ reading numbers in a calculator display
◆ thinking about place value

Equipment
◆ calculators
◆ number cards (0-9, 0-100)
◆ set of decimal cards (several of cards 0-9 and a decimal point card)
◆ 'negative number' cards (showing numbers below 0)
◆ 'calculator' number cards (showing numbers 0-9 as they appear on the buttons and in the display)

Getting started

The children should work in pairs. One child picks a number card and puts that number into the calculator display. Their partner then has to read the number out. Children can take turns doing this, clearing the display each time. (Some children may want to choose their own numbers to enter, instead of using number cards.)

(Very young children could simply work to enter single-digit numbers into the calculator, then match the number in the display with cards showing 'calculator-style' numbers — 4 8 1.)

More confident children can work with cards showing single-digit numbers (or perhaps the set of decimal cards), picking a few and arranging them to make different numbers, then putting these in the calculator display.

Questions to ask the children

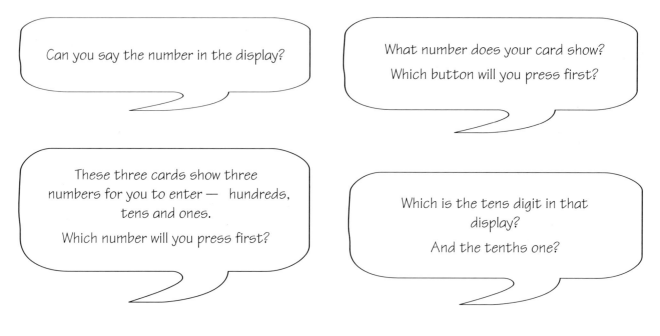

Can you say the number in the display?

What number does your card show?
Which button will you press first?

These three cards show three numbers for you to enter — hundreds, tens and ones.
Which number will you press first?

Which is the tens digit in that display?
And the tenths one?

Keeping going

◆ Children can draw the numbers 0 to 9 as displayed in the calculator — or make them with lengths of straw or sticks.

◆ Children can use dice or spinners to generate numbers.

◆ Children can write down the number their partner has put in the display.

◆ Two children can play *Reducing*. One child enters any number — single-digit to eight-digit — in the calculator. The other child tries to reduce it to 0 by a series of number operations — as few as possible. (Optional rule: in each turn you can press only one number button, though you can press 0 as often as you like.)

◆ Show children the 'Counter' computer program from *Slimwam 2*.

Can the children . . .

match the number on a card to the button on a calculator?

| 0 | 1 | 2 | 3 | 4 | 5 | 6 | 7 | 8 | 9 |

match the number in the display to the correct card from a set showing 'calculator-style' numbers?

0 1 2 3 4 5 6 7 8 9

pre-level 1

read numbers up to at least 10 in the calculator display?

put numbers up to at least 10 in the calculator display according to verbal instructions? (for example 'make it show nine')

level 1

read numbers up to 100 in the calculator display?

put numbers up to 100 in the calculator display according to verbal instructions? (for example, 'make it show thirteen')

find two ways of arranging two single-digit numbers to make two-digit numbers, and read these numbers?

level 2

read whole and decimal numbers up to at least 1000 in the calculator display?

read negative numbers down to at least –1000 in the calculator display?

put any of the above numbers in the calculator display according to verbal instructions? (for example, 'make it show minus fifty-six' or 'make it show five point five')

level 3

MORE OR LESS?

Children will experience

◆ counting objects accurately, using grouping in tens where appropriate

◆ matching numbers with, or making numbers to go with, a set of objects

◆ deciding which of two numbers is more or less than the other

Equipment

◆ number cards (0-10, 0-100)

◆ number tablets 0-9 (several sets)

◆ counters (beads, conkers, cubes . . .)

◆ base ten blocks

◆ straws and rubber bands

◆ 'more/fewer' spinners or dice

Getting started

The children work in pairs. Each child takes a handful of counters and counts them.

(Use larger objects with young children so they do not take more than they can count. If children are working with numbers over 20 you may want them to use base ten apparatus, linking cubes or straws and rubber bands which can easily be grouped in tens.)

Children now use number tablets or cards to make the number which matches their set. They then toss the 'more/fewer' dice to see whether the person with more or with fewer counters is the winner. (Children may want to keep a tally of their scores.)

Questions to ask the children

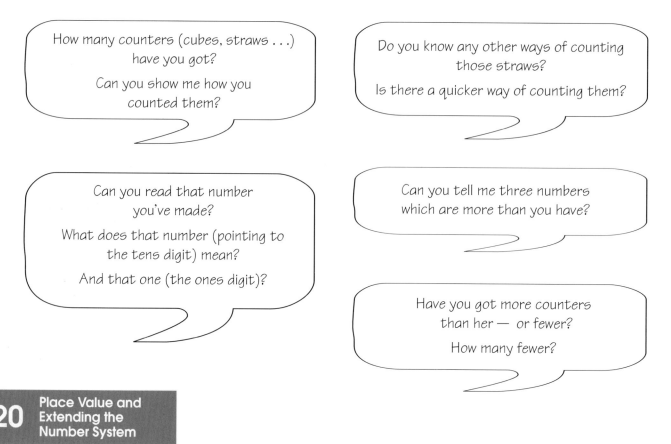

How many counters (cubes, straws . . .) have you got?

Can you show me how you counted them?

Do you know any other ways of counting those straws?

Is there a quicker way of counting them?

Can you read that number you've made?

What does that number (pointing to the tens digit) mean?

And that one (the ones digit)?

Can you tell me three numbers which are more than you have?

Have you got more counters than her — or fewer?

How many fewer?

Keeping going

◆ Young children could match their sets of objects with cards showing arrays of dots instead of numbers.

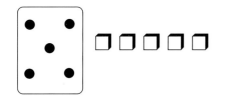

◆ One child puts varying numbers of objects in each of ten pots (a different kind of object in each pot). Their partner estimates the number in each pot and orders them according to the estimates, then checks.

◆ Four children each take a handful of counters (or straws or base ten blocks), arrange them, and put the four collections in order.

Can the children . . .

count a small number of objects?

compare two sets to see which has more or fewer than the other?

understand the words 'more', 'fewer', 'the same' and 'less'?

pre-level 1

count objects up to at least 10?

match objects up to at least 10 with the appropriate number card?

know by looking at the number cards which set has more or fewer counters than the other?

understand and use the words 'more', 'fewer', 'the same' and 'less'?

level 1

count objects up to at least 100, grouping in tens?

match objects up to at least 100 with the appropriate number card?

know by looking at the number cards which set has more or fewer counters than the other?

use single-digit number tablets to make the two-digit number which matches a set of counters?

level 2

count objects up to 1000, grouping in tens and hundreds?

match objects up to 1000 with the appropriate number card?

use single-digit number tablets to make the three-digit number which matches a set of counters?

know by looking at the number cards which set has more or fewer counters than the other?

level 3

CARRY ON

Children will experience

◆ counting and writing numbers
◆ exploring negative numbers
◆ exploring patterns in numbers

Equipment

◆ plain or lined paper
◆ squared paper (perhaps cut into long strips or grids of particular sizes such as 10 x 10 or 2 x 5)
◆ unnumbered number lines
◆ 0-100 grids (for reference)
◆ number lines (for reference)

Getting Started

Give children a number (for example, 0, 1, 50 or 100) and ask them to continue the series of numbers (counting in ones), writing on plain, lined or squared paper or on blank number lines.

Some children could write a series of numbers going backwards, or a series of decimal numbers.

Questions to ask the children

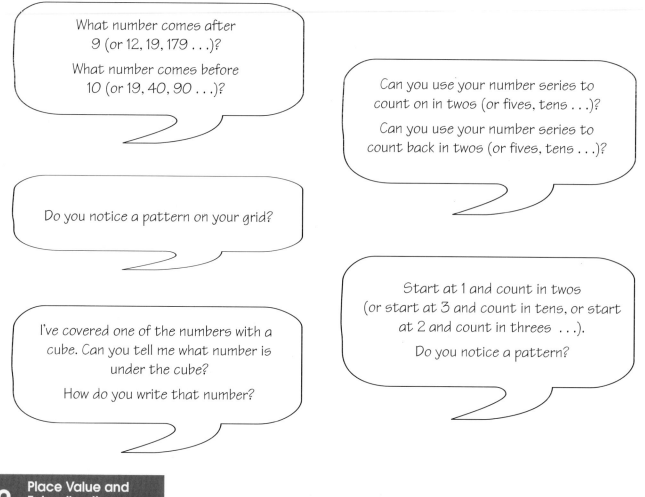

What number comes after 9 (or 12, 19, 179 . . .)?

What number comes before 10 (or 19, 40, 90 . . .)?

Can you use your number series to count on in twos (or fives, tens . . .)?

Can you use your number series to count back in twos (or fives, tens . . .)?

Do you notice a pattern on your grid?

Start at 1 and count in twos (or start at 3 and count in tens, or start at 2 and count in threes . . .).

Do you notice a pattern?

I've covered one of the numbers with a cube. Can you tell me what number is under the cube?

How do you write that number?

Keeping going

◆ If children write their numbers on long strips of squared paper the resulting number tracks could then be used for a variety of games.

◆ Children could record the same number series on number grids of different sizes — for example, 5 x 5, 7 x 10, or 12 x 36. This would show up different number patterns.

◆ You could provide sheets with number sequences for the children to continue.

◆ Children can start off number series for their friends to continue.

Can the children . . .

write down any numbers they know?

attempt to say what those numbers are?

invent symbols for numbers they don't know?

fill in the numbers for birthday cards for other children?

pre-level 1

---

write the numbers to at least 10? attempt those to 20?

find their own way of writing larger numbers? (for example, one hundred and six as `1006')

level 1

---

count, and write the numbers, to at least100?

use a grid to organise their writing?

describe the pattern of the tens numbers?

discuss the pattern of the odd and even numbers?

say and write the numbers past the tens? (for example, 29, 30, 31, . . ., or 78, 79, 80, 81, . . .)

level 2

---

count, and write numbers, to at least1000?

use a grid to organise their writing?

describe the pattern of the tens and hundreds numbers?

count and write the numbers past the tens and hundreds? (for example, 209, 210 , 211, . . . or 499, 500, 501, . . .)

start near or at zero and say and write a series of negative numbers?

write, and read out, a series of decimal numbers to one decimal point?

level 3

Place Value and
Extending the Number System

Fractions and Decimals

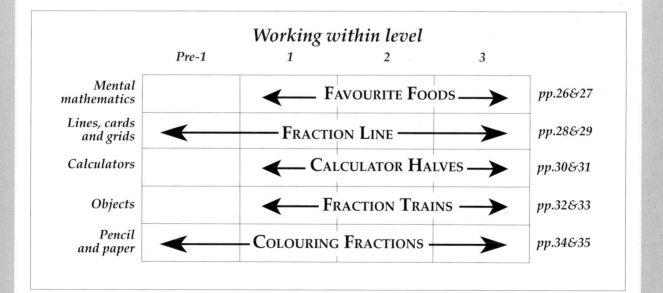

FAVOURITE FOODS

Children will experience

◆ visualising shapes and parts of shapes
◆ visualising numbers of objects and halving those numbers
◆ the language of fractions

Equipment

none needed

Getting started

Ask the chilren to visualise a favourite food treat. Suppose a friend came along and they wanted to share the food with the friend. How could they do that?

Questions to ask the children

What is your food treat?

What shape is that? Can you draw the shape in the air?

What would half of that look like?

Suppose you had an apple (or biscuit/ lolly/chocolate bar). How would you share that with a friend?

What would the two halves look like? Can you draw that?

Suppose you had two biscuits. How would you share those with a friend?

What if you had four biscuits?

What if you had three biscuits? How much would you have each?

Suppose you had a big round cake and three friends (or two, four . . . friends) to share it with. How would you share that fairly?

What shape would your pieces be?

What fraction would you each get?

Suppose I had a big round cake and gave away a quarter. How much would I have left?

Imagine you have ten jam tarts.

Give away half of them.

How many do you have left?

Keeping going

◆ Ask children to draw their favourite food, and then draw what it would look like divided in half — or into other fractions.

◆ Children can make up challenges for each other, such as 'I had twenty football cards and I gave half of them to my friend. How many did he get?'

Can the children . . .

not appropriate *pre-level 1*	draw in the air what their choice of food would look like when shared with a friend? say how much each person will get when a whole is shared between two? (for example, 'she'll get half the cake and so will I') *level 1*
say how much each person will get when a whole is shared between three or four? (for example, 'we'll all get a third') say how much each person will get when a number of objects between 1 and 10 is shared between two people? (for example, 'we'll both get 4 and there's one left over' or 'we'll both get 4 and a half') *level 2*	write a fraction to show how much each person will get when a whole is shared between three or four say how much each person will get when a number of objects (between 1 and 20) is shared between two or more people? (for example, 'we'll all get 6 and a third') *level 3*

FRACTION LINE

Children will experience

◆ writing halves and quarters
◆ thinking about what numbers belong in the 'spaces' between whole numbers

Equipment

◆ unnumbered floor number line with ten or more intervals (this can be drawn in chalk on the floor, in marker pens on a long strip taken from a roll of wallpaper, or made from masking tape on the clear plastic used to protect carpets)
◆ number cards 0-10, 0-20 or 0-30
◆ blank cards and pens
◆ large dice showing 0, 1, 1, 2, 2, 3
◆ large dice showing $1/2$, $1/2$, $1/2$, 1, 1, 1
◆ large dice showing $1/4$, $1/4$, $1/2$, $1/2$, 1, 1

Getting started

This is an activity for a group of four to six chidren, the aim being to put the appropriate number cards on all the markers on the unnumbered line. Ask one child to put the 0 card at the first marker and stand there. The other children take turns tossing the whole-number dice and instruct the child on the line to take that many steps forwards (or backwards, if the dice-thrower chooses) — stepping from marker to marker. Each time the child stops after completing their set of steps, they say what number they are on and put the appropriate number card there.

Having checked that children are familiar with the activity and this way of using a number line, remove the number cards from the line and start again, using the halves-and-wholes dice. The activity is the same, except that the aim is to put in all the half numbers (for example, $3^1/2$) as well as the whole numbers, using the blank cards to write the half numbers.

Some children may be able to work with the dice showing quarters.

Questions to ask the children

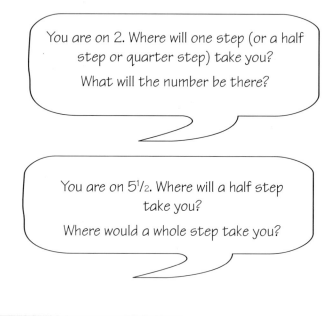

You are on 2. Where will one step (or a half step or quarter step) take you?

What will the number be there?

You are on $5^1/2$. Where will a half step take you?

Where would a whole step take you?

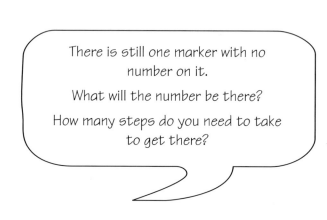

There is still one marker with no number on it.

What will the number be there?

How many steps do you need to take to get there?

Keeping going

◆ Pairs of children can do the same activity using an unnumbered table-top line and writing the numbers on the line.

◆ Children can make a number line from scratch, using whole numbers only, or including fractional numbers as appropriate. If this personalised line is then laminated, they can use it for doing simple calculations.

◆ Children could make up their own games on the fraction line.

Can the children . . .

take steps along a number line, from marker to marker?

count the number of steps they take, up to 5?

pre-level 1

count the number of steps they take, up to 10?

if they know where 0 is, say what number belongs at any of the other markers on an unnumbered line with ten intervals?

on a line numbered 0-10 say how many steps they need to take in order to get from one number to another?

level 1

on a line numbered 0-10 say what number comes halfway between two adjacent numbers? (for example, the number halfway between 3 and 4 is $3\frac{1}{2}$)

on an unnumbered line with ten intervals, place accurately cards showing 0 and whole and half numbers? (for example, place cards 0, $4\frac{1}{2}$ and 5)

make a number line showing whole and half numbers up to 20?

level 2

place cards showing whole, half and quarter numbers in order? (for example, put in order 1, $1\frac{1}{2}$, $1\frac{1}{4}$ and $1\frac{3}{4}$)

make a number line showing whole, half and quarter numbers up to 10?

level 3

CALCULATOR HALVES

Children will experience
◆ exploring the halving of numbers
◆ experience of division
◆ the use of the calculator's constant function

Equipment
◆ calculator
◆ number cards (0-20, 0-100)
◆ number lines
◆ pencil and paper

Getting started

Children work in pairs. They take number cards from the pack and predict what half of that number will be, then use the calculator to find out. Children may do this in several ways:

• by guessing the answer and adding this to itself as a check
• by pressing [÷] [2] [=]
• by using the constant function to set the calculator to divide every number entered by two

You may want to teach children these methods, if they do not think of them themselves.

Encourage children to write down their predictions (on paper or a number line). If children make a rough estimate, 'It will be about . . .', it can help them feel less worried about getting it wrong and so prevent secret rubbing out and rewriting of 'estimates'.

Later, children can experiment with higher numbers of their choice.

Questions to ask the children

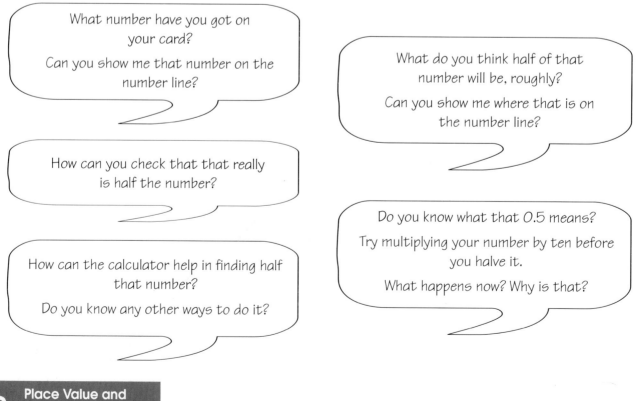

What number have you got on your card?

Can you show me that number on the number line?

What do you think half of that number will be, roughly?

Can you show me where that is on the number line?

How can you check that that really is half the number?

Do you know what that 0.5 means?

Try multiplying your number by ten before you halve it.

What happens now? Why is that?

How can the calculator help in finding half that number?

Do you know any other ways to do it?

Keeping going

◆ Pick numbers at random and halve and double them.

◆ Investigate what happens if they halve even numbers and double odd ones.

◆ When children get answers with a '.5' in them, they can write in these numbers on a number line (for example, putting in 9.5 between the 9 and the 10). They may not fully understand what the decimal number means, but this paves the way for work on decimal lines.

◆ Children can model their numbers with base ten blocks. They will see that some numbers (even ones) divide in half 'cleanly' while others have a remainder of one cube. You can talk with the children about what would happen if the leftover cube were broken up into ten tiny 'flats'. These could be divided up: there would be 5 in each half — a fact which they can link up with the '.5' they have seen in the calculator display.

Can the children . . .

<table>
<tr>
<td>

not appropriate

pre-level 1
</td>
<td>

tell you what 'half' means in the context of sharing something with a friend?

estimate what half of a number up to 10 might be?

level 1
</td>
</tr>
<tr>
<td>

show you a number on the number line to 100 and estimate where half will be?

find a way to check their estimate with a calculator?

say what number is half of any whole number up to 10?

level 2
</td>
<td>

estimate half of any number up to 1000?

check their estimate with a calculator?

say what number is half of any multiple of 10 between 0 and 100?

say what number is half of any multiple of 100 between 0 and 1000?

understand and use the fact that halving is the opposite of doubling?

explain the meaning of 0.5 on the calculator?

level 3
</td>
</tr>
</table>

FRACTION TRAINS

Children will experience

◆ halving a set of cubes
◆ the idea that fractions are a part of a whole
◆ dividing odd and even numbers in half
◆ beginning to think about other fractions, such as thirds and quarters

Equipment

◆ linking cubes such as Multilink or Unifix

Getting started

Children should work in a small group, with you. Ask them to make a 'train' of linking cubes no more than 10 cubes long (though older or more experienced children could move on to making longer ones). They should count the 'carriages' (cubes) and then see if they can break their train exactly in half.

Questions to ask the children

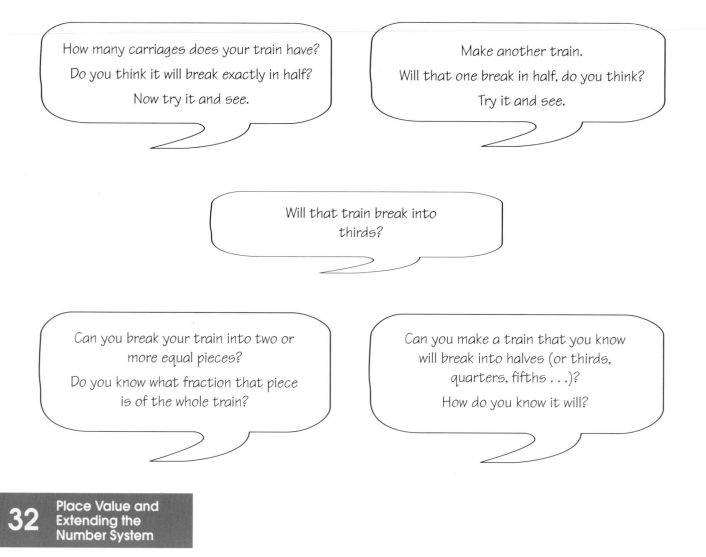

How many carriages does your train have?

Do you think it will break exactly in half?

Now try it and see.

Make another train.

Will that one break in half, do you think?

Try it and see.

Will that train break into thirds?

Can you break your train into two or more equal pieces?

Do you know what fraction that piece is of the whole train?

Can you make a train that you know will break into halves (or thirds, quarters, fifths . . .)?

How do you know it will?

Keeping going

◆ Children can explore systematically trains of lengths from 1 to 10 or 20. Which ones can be halved and which can't? What if you could cut the cubes in half?

◆ Children could mark half of each train-number on a number line and look for patterns.

◆ Ask children to investigate dividing trains up into thirds and quarters, or other equal parts. Are there any lengths of train which won't divide at all?

Can the children . . .

not appropriate
pre-level 1

count accurately the number of carriages up to 10?
find half of a train by trial and error?
say whether or not two parts of a train are equal halves?
level 1

accurately find half of a train that is up to 100 cubes long?
find which trains can be halved and which can't?
talk sensibly about equal lengths?
use and understand the terms 'odd' and 'even'?
level 2

predict how many carriages there will be in half of any train up to 200 carriages long?
use and understand the term 'multiples' in context?
talk sensibly about thirds and quarters?
predict how many carriages there will be in a third or quarter of any train up to 50 carriages long?
level 3

COLOURING FRACTIONS

Children will experience

◆ reading and writing simple fractions
◆ equivalent fractions
◆ addition of simple fractions

Equipment

◆ squared or plain paper
◆ unmarked dice
◆ dice marked 0 1 1 2 3 4
◆ dice marked 0 $\frac{1}{2}$ $\frac{1}{2}$ $\frac{1}{2}$ 1 1
◆ dice marked 0 $\frac{1}{4}$ $\frac{1}{4}$ $\frac{1}{2}$ $\frac{3}{4}$ 1
◆ dice marked 'none, quarter, quarter, half, three quarters, whole'

Getting started

Children should work in groups of two to four. Each child needs four small sheets of paper. They should fold each of these into four equal sections (thus creating a total of sixteen sections per child).

They take turns to toss the dice, read the number and colour in that fraction of one of their sheets of paper. They carry on like this, until everyone has all four pieces coloured in.

Questions to ask the children

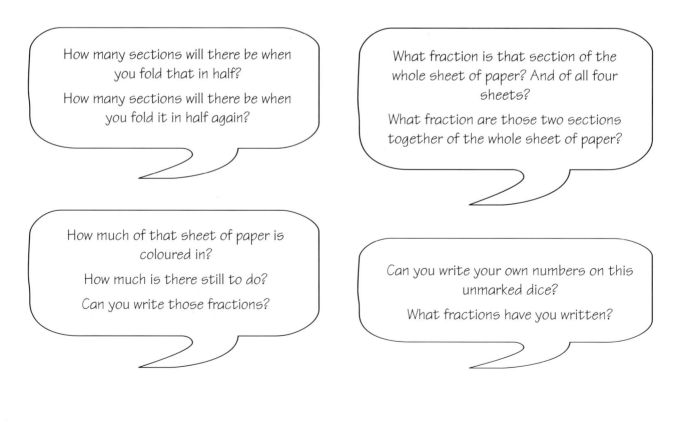

How many sections will there be when you fold that in half?

How many sections will there be when you fold it in half again?

What fraction is that section of the whole sheet of paper? And of all four sheets?

What fraction are those two sections together of the whole sheet of paper?

How much of that sheet of paper is coloured in?

How much is there still to do?

Can you write those fractions?

Can you write your own numbers on this unmarked dice?

What fractions have you written?

Fractions and Decimals: Pencil and Paper

Keeping going

◆ Children could make up their own variations of this game, using more sheets of paper, different fractions . . .

◆ Children could make fraction jigsaw puzzles by cutting a sheet of paper up into pieces — say, a half, a quarter and two eighths — writing the fractions on the pieces, then jumbling them up and reassembling them.

More challenging is to muddle up several such jigsaws, based on different fractions, and reassemble them all.

Can the children . . .

fold a piece of paper in half, and say that it is half?

play the game with one sheet of paper marked into 16 sections, and a dice showing 0, 1 and 2?

pre-level 1

---

fold each piece of paper into two equal sections (thus creating a total of eight)?

say that one section of paper is a half of the whole sheet?

play the game using the dice showing 0, $\frac{1}{2}$ and 1?

level 1

---

fold each piece of paper in half twice?

identify a half and a quarter of one whole sheet?

read the words 'half' and 'quarter'?

write the fractions $\frac{1}{4}$ and $\frac{1}{2}$ and say their names?

level 2

---

fold each piece of paper in half twice?

write fractions such as $\frac{1}{4}, \frac{1}{2}, \frac{2}{4}, \frac{3}{4}, \frac{4}{4}$ and say their names?

identify a half and a quarter of one whole sheet and of all four?

say that each section of the paper is a sixteenth of all four sheets?

say that two quarters are the same as a half?

level 3

Number Relationships and Operations

Pattern

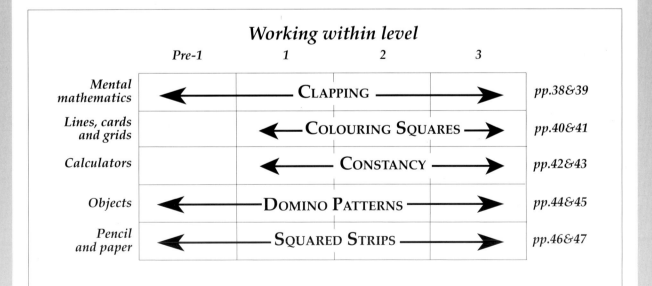

	Working within level				
	Pre-1	*1*	*2*	*3*	
Mental mathematics	←	— Clapping —		→	*pp.38&39*
Lines, cards and grids		← Colouring Squares →			*pp.40&41*
Calculators		← Constancy →			*pp.42&43*
Objects	←	— Domino Patterns —		→	*pp.44&45*
Pencil and paper	←	— Squared Strips —		→	*pp.46&47*

CLAPPING

Children will experience
- Creating, copying and continuing clapping patterns

Equipment
- linking cubes
- pencil and paper
- tape recorder

Getting started

In groups, or with the whole class, the teacher claps a pattern and the children join in — for example, clap hands clap hands, clap knees clap knees, clap hands clap hands, clap knees clap knees, . . .

Questions to ask the children

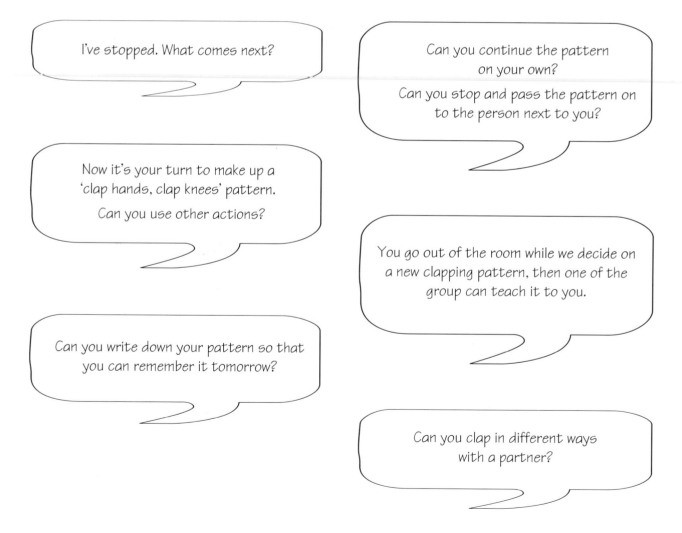

I've stopped. What comes next?

Can you continue the pattern on your own?

Can you stop and pass the pattern on to the person next to you?

Now it's your turn to make up a 'clap hands, clap knees' pattern.

Can you use other actions?

You go out of the room while we decide on a new clapping pattern, then one of the group can teach it to you.

Can you write down your pattern so that you can remember it tomorrow?

Can you clap in different ways with a partner?

Keeping going

◆ Pairs of children can devise patterns for the rest of the class to copy.

◆ Use musical or home-made percussion intruments to create a pattern.

◆ Children can make clapping patterns from their names.

◆ Pairs of children use Unifix cubes in different colours to make the same pattern as the clapping pattern. Then one child points to the Unifix cube row and the other child claps the pattern.

◆ Children can make up patterns with three or more different sounds.

◆ They can make patterns with different rhythms, and work out ways of recording them.

◆ Use a tape recorder to record patterns. Children can listen to the tape and continue the pattern after it has stopped, then make a representation of the taped pattern with linking cubes.

Can the children . . .

join in with a simple rhythmic pattern with no variation?

continue the pattern together without the teacher's help?

pre-level 1

copy a simple rhythm with one variation and repeat it back?

continue a simple clapping pattern with one variation round in a circle?

level 1

copy a rhythm with variation in beats and repeat it back? (for example, step step hop, step step hop, . . .)

continue a pattern with variation in beats round in a circle? (for example, hop hop skip jump, hop hop skip jump, . . .)

invent and continue their own patterns, using different numbers of beats and actions?

find a way of recording their patterns?

level 2

copy a more complex rhythm with different elements and repeat it back? (for example, hands knees ears knees, hands knees ears knees, . . .)

continue a more complex pattern round in a circle? (for example, clap slap click slap, clap slap click slap, clap slap click slap, . . .)

invent and continue their own complex patterns, using different numbers of beats and actions?

find a way of recording their patterns?

level 3

COLOURING SQUARES

Children will experience

◆ exploring number patterns on a number square

◆ becoming familiar with number squares

Equipment

◆ 100-squares, 25-squares, 36-squares

◆ 20-oblongs (4 x 5, 5 x 4 or 10 x 2)

◆ 36-oblongs (showing various arrays)

◆ 100-oblongs (showing various arrays)

◆ other number grids

◆ squared paper

Getting started

Ask the children to colour in 5 and then every 5th square on a number grid. Ask them what patterns they notice. How do they expect the pattern to continue?

Alternatively children can colour in every 3rd, 10th, 7th, square . . .

Or they can colour, say, every 5th number in yellow and every 2nd number in blue stripes.

Questions to ask the children

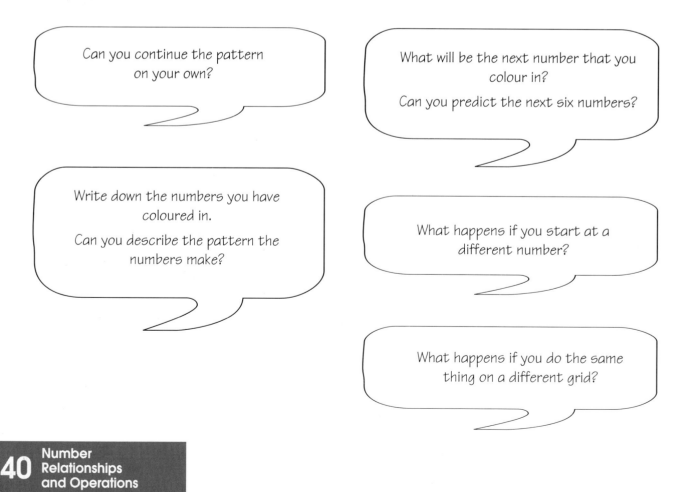

Can you continue the pattern on your own?

What will be the next number that you colour in?

Can you predict the next six numbers?

Write down the numbers you have coloured in.

Can you describe the pattern the numbers make?

What happens if you start at a different number?

What happens if you do the same thing on a different grid?

Keeping going

◆ Ask children to invent a game on a number grid.

◆ Children can explore what happens when colouring in, say, every 5th square on a whole range of number grids. What different patterns can they make?

◆ Ask children to jump in threes on a number square, ringing the numbers they land on. If they say the ringed numbers aloud, can they hear a pattern?

◆ They can jump in fives, threes, twos or nines on a number line. What number patterns do they make?

◆ Or they can make a pattern of jumps on a blank number line and then fill in the numbers.

◆ Children can start at any number on a 0-100 number line, and jump forwards or backwards in tens. Can they say the next number they will land on without looking?

Can the children . . .

not appropriate

pre-level 1

colour in every second square on a number grid to at least 10?

make sensible predictions about which numbers will be coloured in when doing this?

make sensible predictions about which numbers will not be coloured in when doing this?

level 1

colour in every nth square on a number grid to at least 100?

explain what they are doing?

make sensible predictions about which numbers will and will not be coloured in when doing this?

recognise odd and even numbers?

continue the pattern when colouring every nth number starting at, say 1?

spot deliberate mistakes in a pattern?

level 2

continue the pattern when colouring every nth number starting at any number?

explain what they are doing?

make sensible predictions about which numbers will and will not be coloured in when doing this?

spot deliberate mistakes in a pattern?

level 3

CONSTANCY

Children will experience

♦ becoming familiar with simple and more complex number series
♦ predicting and checking predictions
♦ the use of the calculator's constant function
♦ mental calculation

Equipment

♦ calculator
♦ desk-top or overhead-projector calculator
♦ 0-30 or 0-100 number line
♦ 100 squares

Getting started

Use the constant function on the calculator to add or subtract 2, 5, 10 or some other number repeatedly. Children can start at 0 or some other number.

Ask children to guess what the next number in the series will be, and write down this guess, then check.

counting in twos

guess 2 2 6 8 12 13
check 2 4 6 8 10 12

Questions to ask the children

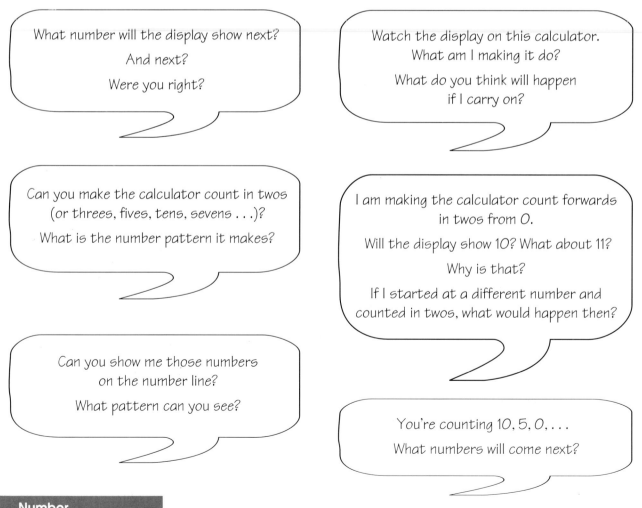

What number will the display show next?

And next?

Were you right?

Watch the display on this calculator. What am I making it do?

What do you think will happen if I carry on?

Can you make the calculator count in twos (or threes, fives, tens, sevens . . .)?

What is the number pattern it makes?

I am making the calculator count forwards in twos from 0.

Will the display show 10? What about 11?

Why is that?

If I started at a different number and counted in twos, what would happen then?

Can you show me those numbers on the number line?

What pattern can you see?

You're counting 10, 5, 0, . . .

What numbers will come next?

Keeping going

◆ Children can do this activity in pairs. One child keys in a secret function and their partner watches the display and tries to predict the next number to appear.

The partner can also try and work out the secret function and the starting number — this can be easier if the child writes down the numbers and looks at them on a number line.

◆ Children could record their calculator 'counts' on number grids or lines. They could then swap their record with a friend who has to try and work out what the 'count' was, and continue the pattern.

◆ You could give children sheets with sequences for them to continue — including negative numbers.

Can the children . . .

not appropriate	count in twos with you, from 0 to at least 10? count with you, in twos, back from 10 to 0?
pre-level 1	*level 1*

predict the next number when the calculator is counting from 0 in twos or fives, up to at least 20? describe the number pattern when the calculator is counting from 0 in twos, fives or tens up to 100? tell you the numbers they won't get when counting in twos or fives from 0 up to at least 20? spot deliberate mistakes in a number pattern?	describe and predict the number pattern made by repeated addition of any single-digit number — whether starting at 0 or another number? spot deliberate mistakes in a number pattern? tell you which numbers will not appear in a given series? (for example, 14 will not appear when counting in threes from 0)
level 2	*level 3*

DOMINO PATTERNS

Children will experience

◆ understanding a pattern intuitively
◆ describing a pattern and its 'rule'
◆ awareness of visual patterns
◆ awareness of number patterns

Equipment

◆ dominoes (one or more sets depending on the number of children)

Getting started

Start making a pattern with the dominoes (they can be face up or face down; you can pay attention to the numbers or not, as suits the children's level of ability). Ask the children to take turns placing the next domino correctly according to the pattern.

Questions to ask the children

What domino comes next?
How do you know?
Can you find that domino?

How should the next domino be arranged?
Can you tell me where exactly to put it?
Can you tell your friend where to put it?

Can you put out the next two dominoes in the pattern?
The next three?

I'm covering up this domino.
Can you say which domino it is?

Can you describe the pattern we are making?

Can you make your own pattern?
Alone or with a friend?

Keeping going

◆ Children can make patterns with sticks of linking cubes, beads on a lace, Lego pieces . . .

◆ Children can make a pattern including a deliberate error and challenge a friend to spot the mistake.

◆ Pairs of children can work together. They each start a pattern off, then swap to complete each other's.

Can the children . . .

continue a simple pattern of dominoes, turned so their numbers are hidden?

pre-level 1

continue or make a simple pattern of dominoes, turned so their numbers are hidden, and describe the pattern?

spot deliberate mistakes in simple patterns such as the one above?

put the domino doubles in order?

level 1

describe and continue or make a pattern of dominoes, based on a simple number sequence such as this?

spot deliberate mistakes in simple number patterns such as the one above?

continue or make a pattern of odd and even numbers?

both even/both odd . . .

level 2

continue or make more complex patterns?

total makes 10, 8, 6, 4 . . .

describe a pattern such as the one above?

spot deliberate mistakes in number patterns such as the one above?

verbalise the 'rule' for a pattern such as the one above?

level 3

SQUARED STRIPS

Children will experience

◆ starting and continuing patterns
◆ describing patterns
◆ finding the 'rule' for a pattern

Equipment

◆ squared paper cut into strips one square wide — the strips can be 6 squares long, 12 squares, 20 squares or more
◆ squared paper cut into strips more than one square wide
◆ coloured pencils or felt-tipped pens

Getting started

Give children each a strip of squared paper and two colours. Ask them to colour the squares according to some pattern. (With younger children you may want to start off the strips yourself and ask them to continue.)

Children may use more than one colour for a square, or decorate rather than colour in the squares. This is fine as long as there is some rule evident.

Questions to ask the children

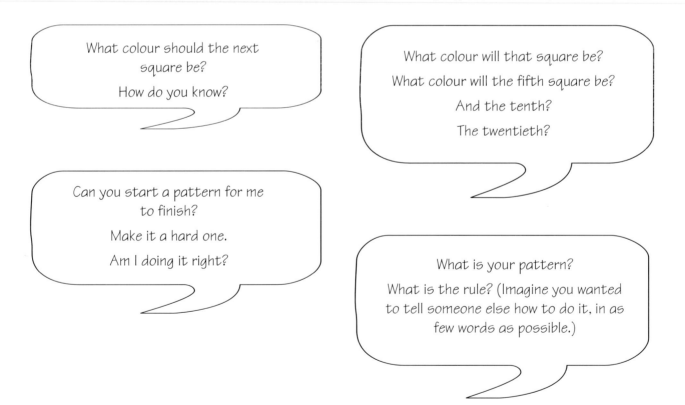

What colour should the next square be?

How do you know?

What colour will that square be?
What colour will the fifth square be?
And the tenth?
The twentieth?

Can you start a pattern for me to finish?

Make it a hard one.

Am I doing it right?

What is your pattern?
What is the rule? (Imagine you wanted to tell someone else how to do it, in as few words as possible.)

Keeping going

◆ Children can colour a single-width strip in alternate colours, then cut this into strips of equal length — say two, three or five squares long — and reassemble them as a rectangle. This produces some interesting patterns.

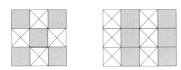

◆ Use blocks or potato pieces to print on fabric or card.

◆ Use numbers instead of colours:

1 2 3 1 2 3
2 3 1 2 3 1

1 2 2 4 1 2 2 4
2 4 1 2 2 4 1 2
1 2 2 4 1, 2 2 4

Can the children . . .

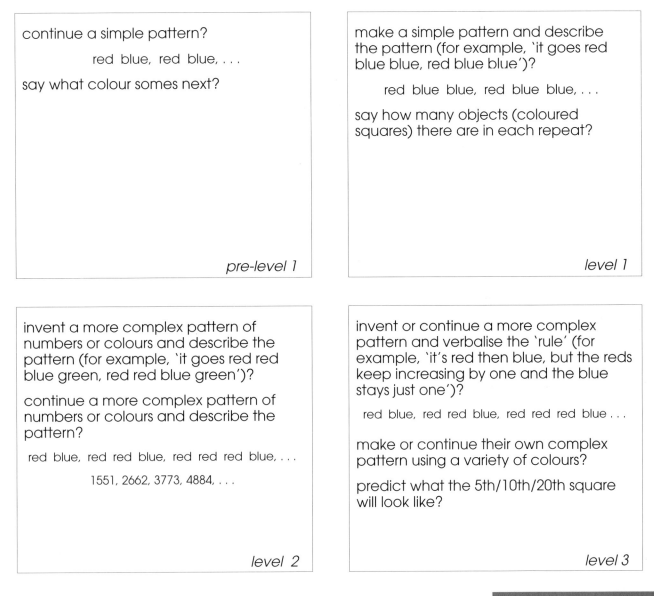

continue a simple pattern?

     red blue, red blue, . . .

say what colour somes next?

pre-level 1

make a simple pattern and describe the pattern (for example, 'it goes red blue blue, red blue blue')?

     red blue blue, red blue blue, . . .

say how many objects (coloured squares) there are in each repeat?

level 1

invent a more complex pattern of numbers or colours and describe the pattern (for example, 'it goes red red blue green, red red blue green')?

continue a more complex pattern of numbers or colours and describe the pattern?

  red blue, red red blue, red red red blue, . . .

    1551, 2662, 3773, 4884, . . .

level 2

invent or continue a more complex pattern and verbalise the 'rule' (for example, 'it's red then blue, but the reds keep increasing by one and the blue stays just one')?

  red blue, red red blue, red red red blue . . .

make or continue their own complex pattern using a variety of colours?

predict what the 5th/10th/20th square will look like?

level 3

Number Relationships and Operations

Operations: Addition and Subtraction

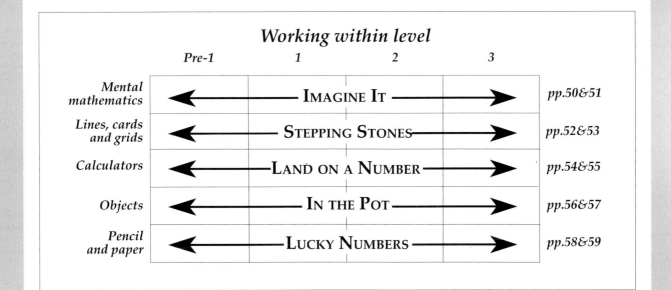

		Working within level		
	Pre-1	*1*	*2*	*3*
Mental mathematics	← ———————— Imagine It ———————— →				pp.50&51
Lines, cards and grids	← ———————— Stepping Stones ———————— →				pp.52&53
Calculators	← ———————— Land on a Number ———————— →				pp.54&55
Objects	← ———————— In the Pot ———————— →				pp.56&57
Pencil and paper	← ———————— Lucky Numbers ———————— →				pp.58&59

49

IMAGINE IT

Children will experience

- developing mental images of small numbers
- developing mental imagery as a way of operating on numbers
- developing strategies for mental calculation

Equipment

- counters or cubes

Getting started

Show the children a few counters in your hand or on the floor/table. Ask the children to close their eyes and picture them in their heads. (You may want to spend some time arranging the counters in patterns, counting them, adding or subtracting one, and so on, all the while encouraging children to close their eyes and imagine the counters.)

Now put away the counters and tell the children to imagine they have each got some counters in their hand. Ask each child in turn how many she or he has got.

Now ask them to take away one (still in imagination) and say how many are left.

Ask them to add two. How many are there?

Go on adding and subtracting like this.

Questions to ask the children

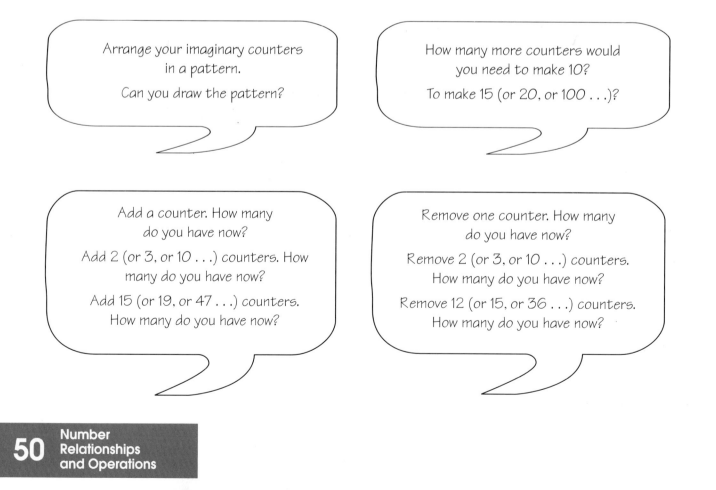

Arrange your imaginary counters in a pattern.

Can you draw the pattern?

How many more counters would you need to make 10?

To make 15 (or 20, or 100 . . .)?

Add a counter. How many do you have now?

Add 2 (or 3, or 10 . . .) counters. How many do you have now?

Add 15 (or 19, or 47 . . .) counters. How many do you have now?

Remove one counter. How many do you have now?

Remove 2 (or 3, or 10 . . .) counters. How many do you have now?

Remove 12 (or 15, or 36 . . .) counters. How many do you have now?

Keeping going

◆ Ask children to imagine a number of counters and, in their heads, arrange them in a pattern. Now ask them to draw the pattern.

Can they rearrange them mentally and draw the new pattern?

◆ Ask children to imagine a number of counters and, in their heads, arrange them in twos. Are there any left over?

Can they arrange them in threes? Are there any left over?

◆ Pairs of children can ... child puts a number o... the table in a pattern. ᴛ⹁ᴇ ᴏⷨ⹁ᴇr person has a good look, then closes their eyes.

The first person hides one or more counters (or adds some). The other person now opens their eyes and tries to work out what has been changed.

Can the children . . .

picture a number of counters and tell you how many there are, up to 5?

picture a number of counters arranged in a pattern, then draw the pattern?

say how many there are after adding one, up to 5?

say how many there are after subtracting one, up to 5?

pre-level 1

imagine some counters, then say how many there are after adding one or two, up to at least 10?

say how many there are after subtracting one or two, up to at least 10?

say how many more counters they would need to make at least 10?

level 1

imagine a number (up to at least 50) and say the total after a number (between 2 and 9) has been added?

imagine a number (up to at least 50) and say what is left after a number (between 2 and 9) has been subtracted?

imagine a number and say what number they would need to add or subtract to make 10, 20, 30 or 50?

level 2

imagine a number and say the total after a number (for example, 12, 23 or 47) has been added?

imagine a number and say what is left after a number (for example, 17, 37 or 54) has been subtracted?

imagine a number and say what number they would need to add or subtract to make 25, 36 or 99?

level 3

Children will experience

- accurately moving forwards and backwards on a blank track or line
- accurately moving forwards and backwards on a numbered line
- exploring different ways of reaching a number from zero
- exploring different ways of moving from one number to another

Equipment

- a floor number track or line — a temporary chalked one will do (for pre-level one you could omit the numbers to start with)
- skittles or bean bags
- (for older children) table top number lines — lines not tracks for this activity, as it is important that children learn the conventions of the number line

Getting started

Floor activity

A group of about four is a good number for working with a floor line or track. Choose a starting point and end point for the (blank or numbered) line or track appropriate to the children's level.

Work with the children on following simple instructions about taking steps along the line.

Table top activity

A group of about four is also a good number for working with a table top number line.

Work with the children on moving from one point to another, making steps (from one marker to an adjacent one) and jumps (worth two or more steps). Help them count the spaces between markers rather than the markers themselves.

Questions to ask the children

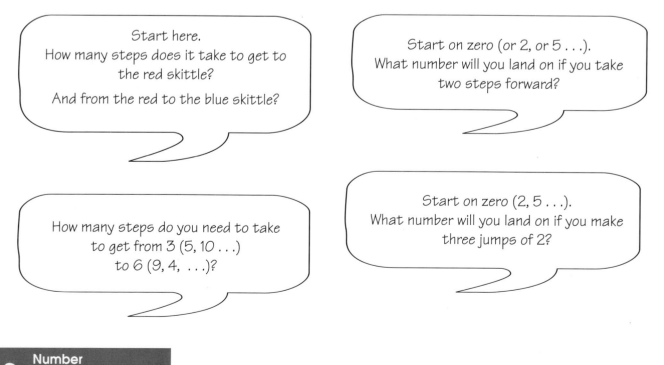

Start here.
How many steps does it take to get to the red skittle?
And from the red to the blue skittle?

Start on zero (or 2, or 5 . . .).
What number will you land on if you take two steps forward?

How many steps do you need to take to get from 3 (5, 10 . . .) to 6 (9, 4, . . .)?

Start on zero (2, 5 . . .).
What number will you land on if you make three jumps of 2?

Keeping going

◆ Explore different ways of getting from 0 to 10 on the floor line using steps and hops — for example 'six steps and four hops'. Try ways of getting from 10 to 0, or from 8 to 1 . . .

◆ *Number Line Nim*
In turns, two children make either a single step or jump of two on a table top number line. The winner is the player to land exactly on 10 (or 20).

◆ *Escape from 10*
This game needs a 0-20 number line, two counters (a bit of blutack on each helps), an operations dice showing + + + − − − , and an ordinary dice.

Both players start on 10. They take it in turns to toss both dice and move forward or backward the appropriate number of steps. The winner is the first to reach either zero or 20.

Can the children . . .

follow simple forward and backward instructions on a blank floor number track?

give each other instructions?

find and stand on a given number on a numbered floor line?

pre-level 1

follow simple forward and backward instructions on a floor number line?

make and count steps accurately on a floor line?

tell you how many steps and the direction they need to take to move from 3 (or 6, 8 . . .) to 7 (or 10, 4 . . .)?

draw or make steps accurately on a table top number line and tell you how many steps they have made?

level 1

draw or make steps or jumps accurately on a table top number line and tell you how many steps their jump is equivalent to?

discover all the ways to reach 20 (or 19, 15, 10 . . .) from 0, using exactly two jumps?

record their two jumps?

level 2

discover all the ways to reach any number up to 100 from 0 with exactly two, five or ten jumps?

record their jumps?

choose a 'start' and 'finish' number and discover all the ways of getting from one to the other in exactly two jumps?

organise their results to check if they have missed any combination?

start at 0 and discover all the ways to reach numbers up to 30 using equal jumps?

level 3

LAND ON A NUMBER

Children will experience

◆ exploring addition and subtraction
◆ developing and using mental strategies for adding and subtracting
◆ familiarity with the calculator

Equipment

◆ calculators
◆ pencils and paper
◆ dice (showing spots or numbers 1-6)
◆ spinners

Getting started

This activity is for two children sharing a calculator. They first set the calculator at 10. Then each child picks a target number under 20 and writes it down (this can either be done in secret, or each child can know the other's target). They then take turns to roll a dice, and choose whether to add or subtract the number shown to the running total in the display. When the calculator displays one of their hidden numbers the game is over.

Children can also work cooperatively. They should start with the calculator set at 0 and choose a number to aim for under 10.

Older or more confident children can use two dice or spinners and choose higher target numbers. Each dice number can be added or subtracted, thus giving four options with each turn. You could also designate one dice as representing 'tens' numbers — 10, 20, 30 and so on.

Questions to ask the children

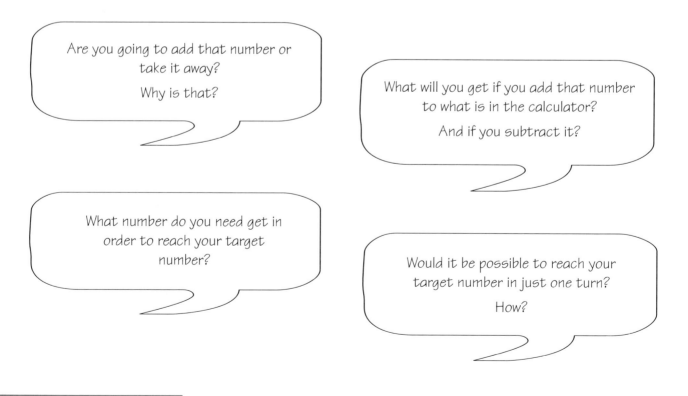

Are you going to add that number or take it away?

Why is that?

What will you get if you add that number to what is in the calculator?

And if you subtract it?

What number do you need get in order to reach your target number?

Would it be possible to reach your target number in just one turn?

How?

Keeping going

◆ Children can explore this game using all kinds of dice and spinners. Which variation do they think makes the best game?

◆ Two children set the calculator at 10, one child operates on that number in secret, and the other tries to guess what buttons were pressed. (Children could use operation cards which tell them what to do, or they could invent their own operations.)

Can the children . . .

key the number that is shown on the dice into the calculator?   *pre-level 1*

add the dice-number to the one shown in the calculator display and read the answer — up to at least 20? subtract the dice-number from the one shown in the calculator display and read the answer — up to at least 20? choose when to add and when to subtract in order to get closer to their target number? *level 1*

add the dice-number to the one shown in the calculator display and read the answer — up to at least 100? subtract the dice-number from the one shown in the calculator display and read the answer — up to at least 100? predict what number will appear in the display when a single-digit number is added or subtracted? *level 2*

predict what number will appear in the display when a two-digit number is added? predict what number will appear in the display when a two-digit number is subtracted?   *level 3*

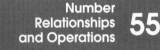

IN THE POT

Children will experience

◆ exploring addition and subtraction facts
◆ developing strategies for determining missing numbers in addition and subtraction problems
◆ developing mental images of small numbers

Equipment

◆ a large yogurt pot
◆ counting objects such as beans or conkers
◆ base ten blocks

Getting started

Choose an appropriate number of beans for the level of the children. Hold the pot in a position so that the children cannot see inside it and put the beans into the pot, one at a time. Do not always count the beans as you place them in the pot. If the children want to count along, encourage them to do so silently.

Ask the children how many beans there are in the pot, then tip the beans out and invite a child to check the number.

Now put all the beans back in the pot and check that the children are clear about how many there are in it. (For pre-level 1 children, you may want to stop here. The activity would then focus on the idea that the number of beans you are working with remains constant, whether or not they are in the pot.)

Add or remove a number of beans from the pot. If putting beans in, clearly show how many you are adding. If removing them, place them in view.

Ask the children to say how many beans are now in the pot.

Questions to ask the children

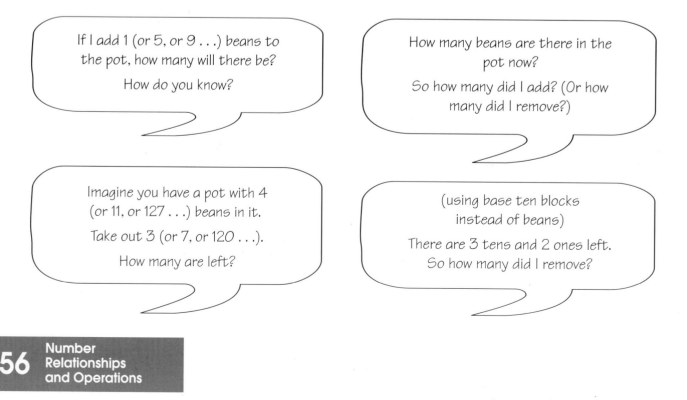

If I add 1 (or 5, or 9 . . .) beans to the pot, how many will there be?

How do you know?

How many beans are there in the pot now?

So how many did I add? (Or how many did I remove?)

Imagine you have a pot with 4 (or 11, or 127 . . .) beans in it.

Take out 3 (or 7, or 120 . . .).

How many are left?

(using base ten blocks instead of beans)

There are 3 tens and 2 ones left. So how many did I remove?

Keeping going

◆ *Spill the Beans*
Children work with a fixed number of beans (or base ten blocks) and take it in turns to tip the pot upside down, spilling some beans (blocks) onto the table and trapping the rest in the pot. They score a point if they can say correctly how many remain in the pot.

◆ Each child in a group has the same number of beans and an A4 piece of paper. Everyone drops their beans (from not too great a height!) onto the paper and in turn describes the groupings formed. For example; 'There is a group of 2, a group of 3 and 1 single bean'. Ask the children to record their groupings in some way.

◆ Provide duplicated copies of a drawing of an up-turned pot. Give the children a fixed number. Ask them to find as many ways as they can to show some beans under the pot and the rest on the table. Talk about how to organise the different pieces of paper and ask the children to stick them onto a larger sheet.

Can the children . . .

tell you how many beans are in the pot for numbers up to five?

check accurately how many beans were in the pot?

tell you that the total number of beans does not change?

solve simple problems involving adding or removing 1 bean?

pre-level 1

tell you how many beans are in the pot for numbers up to at least ten?

check accurately how many beans were in the pot?

solve simple problems involving adding or removing 2 beans?

level 1

find ways to check accurately how many beans were in the pot without counting every one? (for example, knowing that the beans tipped out into a group of 3 and a group of 4 means there were seven in the pot)

solve problems when beans are added or removed as a group? (for example, adding five beans to the pot without counting them in singly)

level 2

find ways to check accurately up to 20 beans without counting every one? (for example, counting the beans two at a time)

solve problems when beans are added or removed as a group, using strategies other than counting on or counting back?

solve problems with base ten blocks when some are added or removed, counting in tens and ones?

level 3

LUCKY NUMBERS

Children will experience

◆ adding and subtracting with concrete objects
◆ exploring the difference between numbers
◆ investigating and recording

Equipment

◆ dominoes (a complete or incomplete set)
◆ sets of double-nine or double-twelve dominoes
◆ number cards 0 to 9

Getting started

Work in a group of your choice.

At all levels the children start with a set of dominoes. Ask the children to count the spots and see if they notice anything.

Questions to ask the children

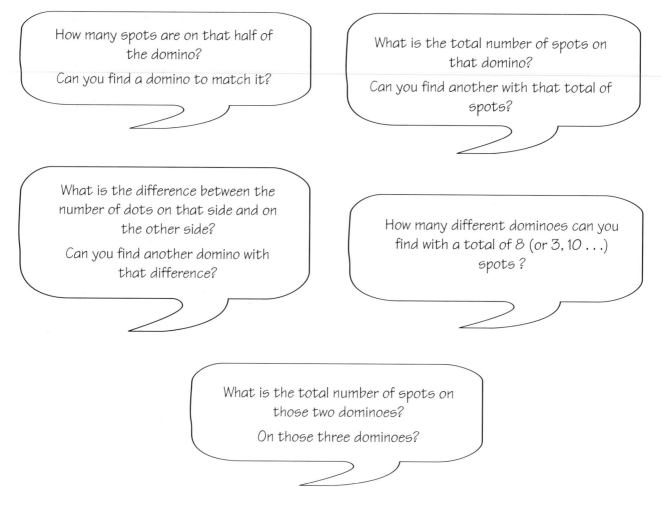

How many spots are on that half of the domino?

Can you find a domino to match it?

What is the total number of spots on that domino?

Can you find another with that total of spots?

What is the difference between the number of dots on that side and on the other side?

Can you find another domino with that difference?

How many different dominoes can you find with a total of 8 (or 3, 10 . . .) spots ?

What is the total number of spots on those two dominoes?

On those three dominoes?

Keeping going

◆ *Domino Bingo*
Four children share out a set of dominoes, then take turns to toss two dice and announce the total. Any player with a domino (or dominoes) with an equivalent number of spots turns it (them) face down. The winner is the first person to turn all their dominoes face down.

◆ Children take a domino and make pairs of two- or one-digit numbers — for example, a three/five domino produces 35 or 53, a double three makes 33 and 33, one-zero makes 1 (01) and 10.

Ask children to add the numbers in each pair together. What do they notice?

Can the children . . .

tell you the number of spots on one half of a domino?

make a domino chain by matching spots?

pre-level 1

choose a domino and add the two numbers together?

find other dominoes with the same totals?

subtract the number on one half from the number on the other half?

find other dominoes with equivalent differences?

level 1

choose a domino, add the two numbers and say what other dominoes there should be which add up to the same amount (without looking)?

choose a domino, find the difference between the two numbers and say what other dominoes there should be with that same difference (without looking)?

choose any two dominoes and find the total number of spots without counting?

level 2

choose any three or four dominoes and find the total number of spots without counting?

find ways of making all the numbers from 1 to 20 using two dominoes?

find a way of recording what they have done?

work out which dominoes are missing from a set?

level 3

Operations: Multiplication and Division

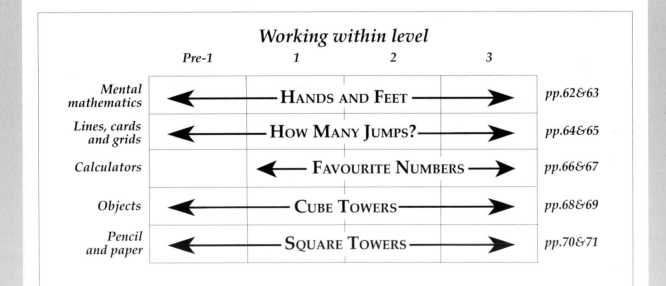

	Working within level				
	Pre-1	*1*	*2*	*3*	
Mental mathematics	←	HANDS AND FEET		→	*pp.62&63*
Lines, cards and grids	←	HOW MANY JUMPS?		→	*pp.64&65*
Calculators		←	FAVOURITE NUMBERS	→	*pp.66&67*
Objects	←	CUBE TOWERS		→	*pp.68&69*
Pencil and paper	←	SQUARE TOWERS		→	*pp.70&71*

HANDS AND FEET

Children will experience

◆ exploring multiplication facts
◆ developing mental images of multiplication
◆ developing the idea that multiplication is equivalent to repeated addition

Equipment

none needed

Getting started

Multiplication

Ask children: How many hands have you got each? How many hands have two of you got? Three of you? Four of you?

How many hands and feet have you got each? How many hands and feet have two of you got? Three of you? Four of you?

(The children may need time to count before answering the questions.)

Carry on asking multiplication questions like this, increasing the complexity as appropriate. Harder questions might include: How many fingers have five of you got altogether? How many toes on eight people? Everybody hide their thumbs and little fingers; how many fingers are showing now in the group?

Division

Ask children: There are six hands in the room; how many people are there? There are twenty fingers showing; how many people is that?

Carry on asking division questions like this, increasing the complexity as appropriate.

Questions to ask the children

How many toes are there on one person?

On two people? On three people?

Can you write those numbers?

How many hands are there on one person?

On two people? Three people?

Ring those numbers on the number line.

There are six hands in the group. How many people is that?

How can you work that out?

There are twenty toes in the group. How many people is that?

How did you work that out?

Keeping going

◆ Children can make sets of hand prints showing their fingers clearly, and record the number of fingers showing. A group of children could make a display showing a series of pictures from one hand to ten hands.

◆ Invent monsters with strange numbers of legs or eyes, and work out how many legs one, two, three or more monsters would have.

◆ Investigate sets of wheels on cars, legs on spiders, corners on squares, and so on.

Can the children . . .

tell you how many hands and feet they have?

tell you how many fingers they have on one hand?

pre-level 1

tell you how many fingers they have on both hands?

say how many hands there are in a group of 2, 3, 4 or 5 people?

when counting pairs of hands, find the relevant numbers on a number line?

count in twos up to at least 10?

level 1

count in twos up to at least 20?

count in tens up to at least 30?

count in fives up to at least 25?

count in threes and fours up to at least 24?

say how many twos there are in 20?

say how many tens there are in 30?

say how many fives there are in 25?

level 2

count in tens up to at least 100?

count in fives up to at least 100?

count in threes, fours and other single-digit numbers up to near 50?

say how many fives or tens there are in 35 (or 70. 85, 90 . . .)?

say how many threes there are in any number up to 30?

say how many fours (or sixes, sevens, eight or nines) there are in any number up to 40?

level 3

HOW MANY JUMPS?

Children will experience

◆ accurately moving forwards and backwards on an unnumbered line using equal jumps

◆ accurately moving forwards and backwards on a numbered line using equal jumps

◆ exploring different ways of reaching a number from zero in equal jumps

Equipment

◆ a floor number line — a temporary chalked number line will do (for pre-level one you may wish to omit the numbers and use coloured markers or skittles instead)

◆ table top number lines (0-10, 0-30 or 0-100)

Getting started

Floor activity:

A group of about four is best when working with a floor line. Work with the children on following simple instructions for making jumps worth one or two along the line — moving themselves, or working with plastic figures.

Table top activity:

Work with the children on moving from one point to another, making equal sized jumps (worth two or more) and helping them count the number of jumps.

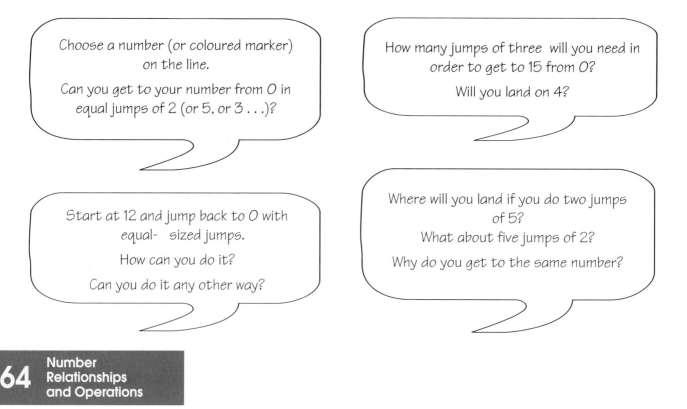

(Children will need to be familiar with the idea of making steps worth one on the number line before doing this activity.)

Questions to ask the children

Choose a number (or coloured marker) on the line.

Can you get to your number from 0 in equal jumps of 2 (or 5, or 3 . . .)?

How many jumps of three will you need in order to get to 15 from 0?

Will you land on 4?

Start at 12 and jump back to 0 with equal- sized jumps.

How can you do it?

Can you do it any other way?

Where will you land if you do two jumps of 5?

What about five jumps of 2?

Why do you get to the same number?

Keeping going

◆ *Number Line Challenge (for 2 children)*
The children choose a number less than 30 on a number line and circle it. The first child scores one point if they can choose a size of jump that will allow them to land exactly on that number, jumping from 0 — they make their prediction and then make the jumps.

The other child scores *two* points if they can predict a different sized jump that also works. Four points go to the first player if they can predict another size of jump that will work, and so on.

When that number is exhausted, the children choose a new one.

Can the children . . .

follow simple forward and backward instructions for jumps sized 1 or 2 on an unnumbered floor line?

give each other instructions?

attempt to say the names of the numbers they land on when using a numbered floor line?

pre-level 1

follow simple forward and backward instructions for jumps sized 1 or 2 on a numbered floor line?

tell you how many jumps of 2 they will take in moving from 0 to 6 (or 8, 10 . . .)?

draw or make equal-sized jumps accurately on a table top line?

level 1

draw or make equal-sized jumps accurately on a table top line and tell you how many jumps they have made?

choose a number below 30 and explore all the ways to reach it from zero in equal-sized jumps?

start on a number below 30 and explore all the ways to get back to zero in equal-sized jumps?

record their equal jumps?

level 2

choose a number below 100 and explore all the ways to reach it from zero in equal-sized jumps?

start on a number below 100 and explore all the ways to get back to zero in equal-sized jumps?

find a way to record their results?

predict what number they will land on if they do 3 (or 5, 10 . . .) jumps of 4 (or 3, 2 . . .)

level 3

FAVOURITE NUMBERS

Children will experience
◆ reading and ordering numbers
◆ exploring number patterns
◆ investigating the relationship between doubling and multiplying by two
◆ investigating the relationship between halving and dividing by two
◆ simple multiplication and division patterns

Equipment
◆ calculators (either one for each child or one between two)
◆ pencil and paper
◆ large sheet of paper (or flip chart) and felt pen

Getting started

Work with a group and ask each child what their favourite number is. Can they get their calculator to show it? As a group, put the calculators in order according to the numbers displayed, then record all the numbers.

Help the children use the addition key to add each number to itself and record the results.

Later, ask the children to multiply each number by two and record the results.

With more experienced children an effective approach is to work with eight children and get them to work in pairs. As a group, collect all the favourite numbers and record them. Then one pair multiplies each of these numbers by 2, another pair adds each number to itself, another pair multiplies each one by 10, and the last divides them by 10.

The pairs explain to the rest of the group what they have noticed. Each pair then explores the operations the others were given.

Questions to ask the children

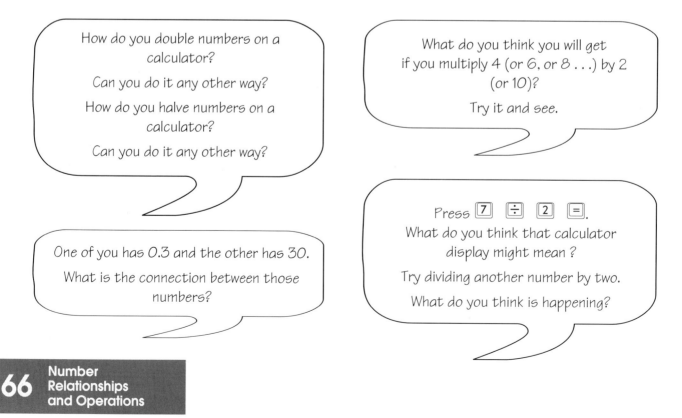

How do you double numbers on a calculator?

Can you do it any other way?

How do you halve numbers on a calculator?

Can you do it any other way?

What do you think you will get if you multiply 4 (or 6, or 8 . . .) by 2 (or 10)?

Try it and see.

One of you has 0.3 and the other has 30.

What is the connection between those numbers?

Press 7 ÷ 2 =.
What do you think that calculator display might mean ?

Try dividing another number by two.

What do you think is happening?

Keeping going

◆ *Beat the Calculator*
Children work in pairs with a pack of cards 1 to 10 and a calculator. They decide on an operation such as 'multiplying by 2' and which of them will use the calculator (the other works in their head). They turn over cards one at a time and operate on that number, each child using their own method. The first to get the answer scores a point. Swap round when all ten cards have been turned over.

◆ Ask the children to investigate which numbers give a whole number answer when divided by 2 on the calculator.

Can the children . . .

not appropriate	add numbers up to 10 to themselves on the calculator? talk about what happens to numbers when they are added to themselves?
pre-level 1	*level 1*
describe how to multiply any number by 2 on the calculator? explain the relationship between doubling, multiplying by 2 and adding a number to itself? explain what happens when a single-digit number is multiplied by 10 on the calculator?	explain how to multiply any number by 10 with or without a calculator? predict the result of multiplying any of the numbers 2, 3, 4 or 5 by 2, 3, 4 or 5? explain the effect of dividing any number by 2 or by 10?
level 2	*level 3*

CUBE TOWERS

Children will experience

◆ developing the idea of 'equal sets'.
◆ exploring ways of dividing up a set
◆ developing mental images of multiplication and division
◆ learning multiplication bonds

Equipment

◆ large wooden cubes
◆ linking cubes
◆ pencil and paper

Getting started

Children take a handful of cubes and try to arrange them in towers of equal height. Encourage them to record their work.

With younger children, or when using higher numbers, you could ask them to make sticks of linking cubes, as towers might be unstable.

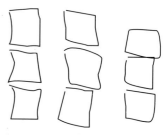

I had 9 cubes.
I made 3 towers of 3.

Questions to ask the children

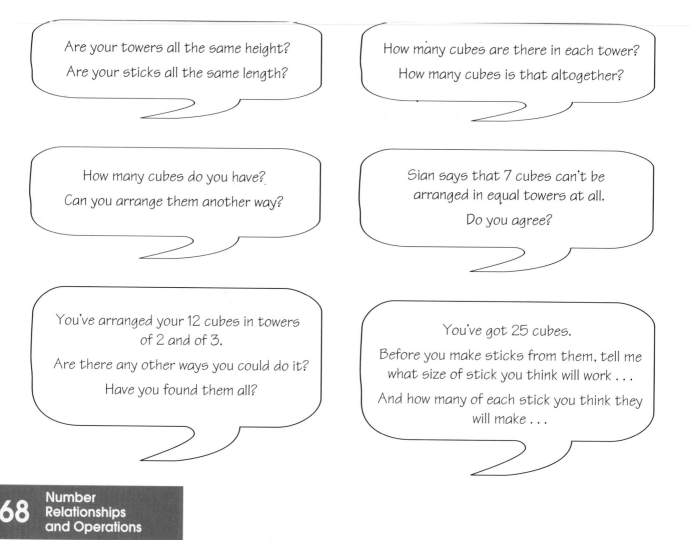

Are your towers all the same height?
Are your sticks all the same length?

How many cubes are there in each tower?
How many cubes is that altogether?

How many cubes do you have?
Can you arrange them another way?

Sian says that 7 cubes can't be arranged in equal towers at all.
Do you agree?

You've arranged your 12 cubes in towers of 2 and of 3.
Are there any other ways you could do it?
Have you found them all?

You've got 25 cubes.
Before you make sticks from them, tell me what size of stick you think will work . . .
And how many of each stick you think they will make . . .

Keeping going

◆ Children could decide on a fixed number of towers and mark tower bases on a sheet of paper. They can then use number cards to tell them the number of cubes to work with, recording which numbers work and which don't.

◆ Children could use the tower bases described above to investigate systematically which numbers can be divided into a given number of equal parts.

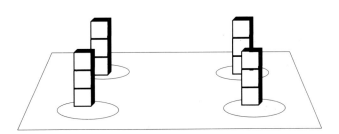

Can the children . . .

share out a small number of cubes between two people — 'one for me, one for you, one for me . . .'?

notice when there is one left over and the sharing is not 'fair'?

pre-level 1

share out at least 10 cubes between two or three people — 'one for me, one for you, one for me . . .'?

count the cubes in a stick and say if the number is the same as, or more, or less than, the number of cubes in another stick?

level 1

work with up to 100 cubes to make towers of equal height, or sticks of equal length?

count how many cubes are in each tower, and find the total number of cubes, up to 100 in number?

look for more than one way of making equal height towers or equal length sticks from a set of cubes?

level 2

say whether any given number of cubes will make towers 2, 5 or 10 cubes high, before making the towers?

say whether any given number of cubes up to 25 will make equal towers, before making the towers?

be systematic in looking for all the ways of making equal height towers from a set of cubes?

talk about numbers of cubes that can't be divided up fairly, and why this is?

level 3

SQUARE TOWERS

Children will experience

◆ exploring multiplication facts
◆ developing mental images of multiplication and division
◆ developing the idea of 'equal sets'
◆ exploring ways of dividing up a set
◆ learning multiplication bonds
◆ recording the results of multiplication

Equipment

◆ squared paper
◆ coloured pens or pencils
◆ dice with spots
◆ dice with numbers

Getting started

In this activity children draw towers of equal height on squared paper and make a written record to go with them.

Ask the children to toss a dice to decide how many squares tall their towers are to be, and draw one tower of that height. Ask them to toss the dice again to see how many towers they are to draw (including the one they have just done).

Children should then make a written record of their work according to their level.

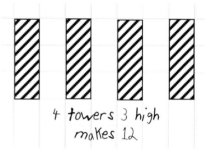

4 towers 3 high makes 12

Questions to ask the children

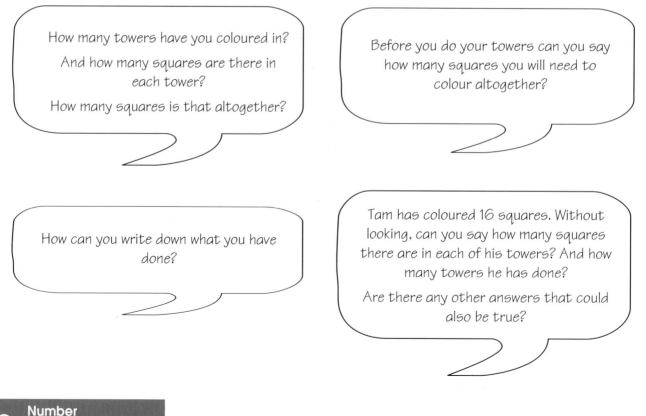

How many towers have you coloured in?

And how many squares are there in each tower?

How many squares is that altogether?

Before you do your towers can you say how many squares you will need to colour altogether?

How can you write down what you have done?

Tam has coloured 16 squares. Without looking, can you say how many squares there are in each of his towers? And how many towers he has done?

Are there any other answers that could also be true?

Keeping going

◆ Children can toss a dice, say the number, and draw a layer of patterned 'wall' that many squares long on squared paper. They then toss the dice again to determine how many layers of the wall they are to draw, one on top of the other.

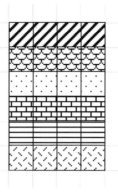

◆ Get children to devise challenges for each other based on their work — 'I drew 5 towers, and I used 20 squares altogether. How tall were they?'

Can the children . . .

draw a tower by colouring a number of squares corresponding to the dots on a normal dice?

draw a tower by colouring a number of squares corresponding to the numerals on a dice, up to 6?

copy a tower by drawing another one of not more than 6 squares?

pre-level 1

draw the right number of towers of the right height, as indicated by the spots or numerals on the dice?

count the squares in a tower and say if the number is the same as, or more or less than, the number of squares in another tower?

count the total number of squares, up to at least 10?

make a simple record of the number of squares in each tower?

level 1

find the total number of squares in their towers, up to at least 100?

count in twos, fives and tens?

make a record of their work — as repeated addition and as multiplication?

$$4 + 4 + 4 = 12$$
$$4 \times 3 = 12$$

level 2

predict the total number of squares in a set of towers (up to 10 in number) that are 2, 5 or 10 squares high, before making the towers?

predict the total number of squares in a set of towers (up to 5 in number) that are up to 5 squares high, before making the towers?

make a record of their work — as repeated subtraction and as division?

$$12 - 4 - 4 - 4 = 0$$
$$12 \div 3 = 4$$

level 3

Number Facts

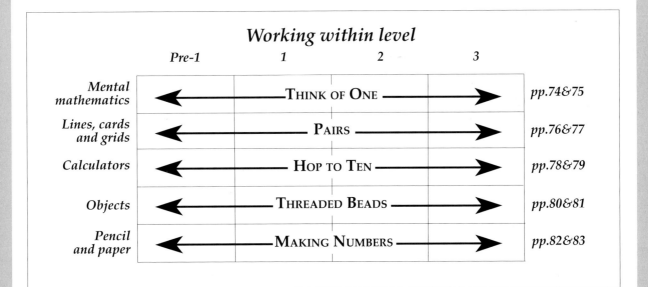

THINK OF ONE

Children will experience

◆ mental addition, subtraction and simple multiplication and division

◆ awareness of number patterns

◆ developing mental imagery

Equipment

none needed

Getting started

Addition and multiplication

Ask children to think of one object (an apple, a counter, a penny . . .). 'Add another one. How many do you have now? . . . And another. How many now?' Get the children to keep adding one, and telling you the answers.

Ask children to think of one object. 'Add two more. How many is that?' 'Add another three. How many is that?' 'Add another four. How many is that?' And so on.

Ask children to think of one object. 'Double it. Keep doubling. How far can you go?'

Ask children to think of two objects. 'Now put two objects like those at each corner of a sheet of paper. How many are there altogether?'

Subtraction and division

Ask children to start with an image of ten objects. 'Remove one of them. How many are left? . . . Remove another one. How many are left now?' Get the children to keep subtracting one, and telling you the answers.

Ask children to start with fifty. 'Subtract five. How many are left? . . . Remove another five. How many are left now?' Get the children to keep subtracting five, and telling you the answers.

Do this again with children subtracting ten each time, or halving their number each time.

Ask children to start with six objects. 'Can you share them out between three children? How many do they each get? . . . Can you share them out between two children?'

Questions to ask the children

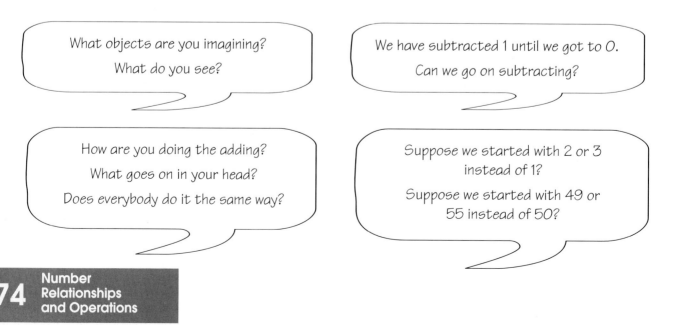

What objects are you imagining?

What do you see?

We have subtracted 1 until we got to 0.

Can we go on subtracting?

How are you doing the adding?

What goes on in your head?

Does everybody do it the same way?

Suppose we started with 2 or 3 instead of 1?

Suppose we started with 49 or 55 instead of 50?

Keeping going

◆ Children can draw what they 'see' in their mind's eye.

◆ Children work in pairs. One person decides on the starting number and the other chooses what operation to do — for example, subtracting two, or doubling. They then work together to take the series as far as they can — perhaps using a calculator.

◆ Children can generate a series of numbers, either mentally or using a calculator, and write the numbers on paper. Another child has to try and work out what operation they were using and continue it.

> 5 7 9 11 13 15 17
> 19 21
> Can you go on
> with this?

Can the children . . .

start at 1 and keep adding 1 up to 5?

start at 5 and keep subtracting 1 to 0?

pre-level 1

start at 1 and keep adding 1 up to at least 10?

start at 10 (at least) and keep subtracting 1 to 0?

level 1

start at 1 or another single-digit number and add 1, then 2, then 3, and so on, up to near 50?

start at 1 and keep doubling, up to 64?

start at 50 and keep subtracting fives to 0?

start at any two-digit number and keep subtracting tens to near 0?

level 2

start at 1 or another single-digit number and add 1, then 2, then 3, and so on, up to near 100?

start at 1 and keep doubling, up to 128?

start at 50 and keep subtracting fives to –50?

start at any two-digit number and keep subtracting tens to near –50?

level 3

PAIRS

Children will experience

- adding numbers to make ten or twenty
- looking for all the ways of making ten or twenty by adding whole numbers
- finding the differences between pairs of numbers
- being systematic

Equipment

- a set of ten cards showing arrays of dots from 1 to 10
- number cards 0-10, with two 5s
- number cards 0-20, with two 10s
- number cards 0-30, with two 15s
- counters
- calculators
- number lines

Getting started

Ask the children to spread the set of cards out in front of them and find pairs of cards whose numbers total 10 (or 20).

They could then look for pairs totalling 9 (or 6, or 18 . . .).

They could also look for pairs with a difference of 10 (or 5, or 9 . . .).

Questions to ask the children

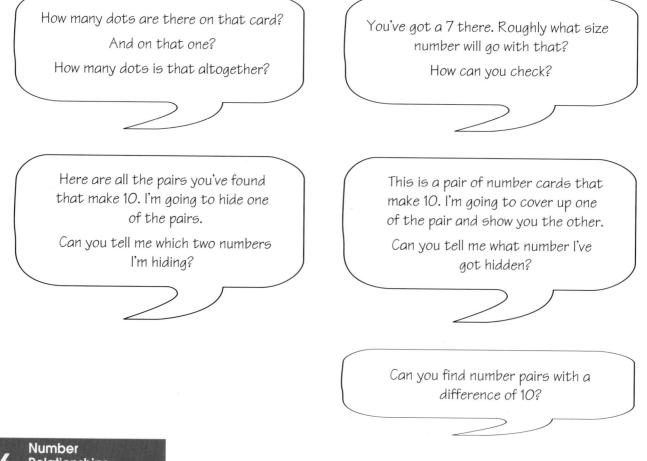

How many dots are there on that card?

And on that one?

How many dots is that altogether?

You've got a 7 there. Roughly what size number will go with that?

How can you check?

Here are all the pairs you've found that make 10. I'm going to hide one of the pairs.

Can you tell me which two numbers I'm hiding?

This is a pair of number cards that make 10. I'm going to cover up one of the pair and show you the other.

Can you tell me what number I've got hidden?

Can you find number pairs with a difference of 10?

Keeping going

◆ Children can put their card pairs in order and then record their work.

> Pairs that make 10
> 10 and 0   9 and 1
> 8 and 2   7 and 3
> 6 and 4   5 and 5

◆ Children can think of as many ways as they can of making 10 — including subtraction, multiplication and division.

◆ Children can make their own set of number cards 0-30 and find number pairs that make 30.

Can the children . . .

---

put cards showing arrays of dots from 1 to 5 in order?

put cards numbered 1-5 in order?

using cards 1-5, say which numbers are higher than other numbers? (for example '4 is more than 1' '2 is higher than 1')

pre-level 1

---

put cards showing arrays of dots from 1 to 10 in order?

find pairs of cards whose dots total 10?

put the cards numbered 0-10 in order?

using cards 0-10, say which numbers are higher than other numbers? (for example '9 is more than 0' '8 is higher than 7')

level 1

---

using cards 0-20, find all possible pairs of cards which total 20, including 0 and 20?

using cards 0-20, find all possible pairs of cards which total 19 (or 18, or 17 . . .)?

arrange these pairs of cards according to a system in order to check that they are all there?

using cards 0-20, find pairs of cards whose difference is 10 (or 15, or 8 . . .)?

level 2

---

using cards 0-30, find all possible pairs of cards which total 30?

using cards 0-30, find all possible pairs of cards which total 29 (or 25, or 23 . . .)?

arrange these pairs of cards according to a system in order to check that they are all there?

using cards 0-30, find pairs of cards whose difference is 20 (or 18, or 7 . . .)?

level 3

HOP TO TEN

Children will experience

◆ thinking about number pairs that make 10
◆ thinking about the effect of each of the four operations
◆ developing strategies

Equipment

◆ calculators
◆ number cards 0-9
◆ number lines

Getting started

In this activity children pick a number between 0 and 9 at random and put that number in the display of their calculator. They then use 'hops' to get from that starting number to a given target. Each hop may use only an operation button ($\boxed{+}$ $\boxed{-}$ $\boxed{\times}$ or $\boxed{\div}$), a *single-digit number* and the $\boxed{=}$ button.

Hop to Ten — for early levels

The aim is to get to ten in one 'hop'. (At this level the only operation children will need to do is adding.)

Two Hops to Twenty — for early and higher levels

The aim is to get from to 20 in two 'hops'. (At higher levels children can be encouraged to use multiplication as well as addition.)

Three Hops to a Hundred — for higher levels

The aim is to get to 100 in three 'hops'. (At this level children can be encouraged to use the full range of operations.)

My hop from
2 to 10

2 + 8 = 10

My hop from
2 to 20

2 + 8 = 10
10 × 2 = 20

My hop from
2 to 100

2 + 8 = 10
10 × 2 = 20
20 × 5 = 100

Questions to ask the children

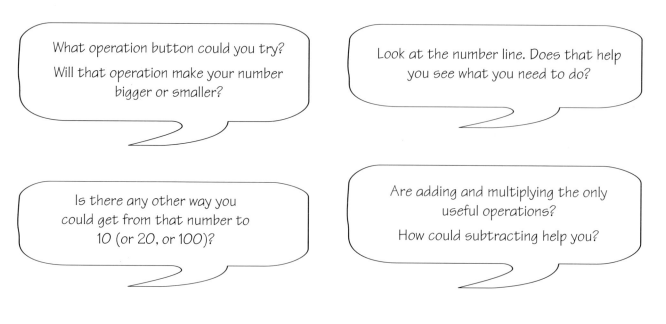

What operation button could you try?

Will that operation make your number bigger or smaller?

Look at the number line. Does that help you see what you need to do?

Is there any other way you could get from that number to 10 (or 20, or 100)?

Are adding and multiplying the only useful operations?

How could subtracting help you?

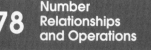

Keeping going

◆ Children can try reaching 10 in one hop from starting points anywhere in the range 0-20 — some hops, such as 15 to 10, will require children to use subtraction.

◆ Children can try reaching 20 in two hops from starting points anywhere in the range 0-50.

◆ Children can try hopping to other numbers such as 9, 15 or 50.

◆ Ask the children whether it is always possible to reach 10 from a single-digit number in just one hop. How do they know?

Similarly, can they always reach 20 from a single-digit number in just two hops? (The answer is 'yes'.)

And can they always reach 100 from a single-digit number in just three hops? (The answer is again 'yes'.)

Can the children . . .

<table>
<tr>
<td>

copy any number from cards numbered 1-5 into the calculator display?

read any number from 1-5 in the calculator display?

pre-level 1
</td>
<td>

copy any number from cards numbered 0-9 into the calculator display?

read any number from 1-9 in the calculator display?

use trial and error on the calculator to get from any single-digit number to 10 by adding?

level 1
</td>
</tr>
<tr>
<td>

read any number from 1-100 in the calculator display?

say how to get from any single-digit number to 10 by adding, and then use the calculator to check?

work out how to get from any single-digit number to 20 by adding and multiplying single-digit numbers, and then use the calculator to check? (for example, 6 – 1 → 5; 5 x 4 → 20)

level 2
</td>
<td>

work out how to get from any single-digit number to 100 by using whichever operations are appropriate and single-digit numbers, and then use the calculator to check? (for example, 3 + 7 → 10; 10 x 5 → 50; 50 x 2 → 100)

level 3
</td>
</tr>
</table>

THREADED BEADS

Children will experience

◆ thinking about number pairs that make a given total

◆ thinking about equal sets

◆ using mental imagery to solve number problems

◆ recording addition and subtraction operations

Equipment

◆ coloured beads

◆ laces

Getting started

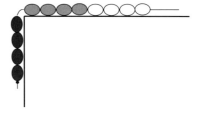

You should work with a group of about four children. Get one of the children to thread up to 10 beads, all the same colour, on a lace. (Let the children thread the beads as this gives them a sense of 'ownership' of the beads and so of the numbers.) You then take the lace and hang it over the edge of the table so that some of the beads are hidden. Ask the children to tell you how many are hidden, then let them count to check. Now let one of them hide some of the beads (but keeping the same total).

You can later work with more beads on the lace — make sure each full ten is in a different colour so that counting the number of beads showing and hidden is relatively easy.

You can also work with sets of beads on a lace — for example, three sets of four with each four in a different colour. In this case, hide one or more complete sets at a time and ask the children 'How many sets are missing? How many beads is that?'

Questions to ask the children

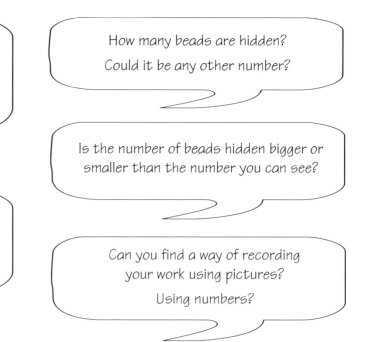

How many beads are there altogether on the lace?

And how many can you see?

So how many are hidden?

How many beads are hidden?

Could it be any other number?

Is the number of beads hidden bigger or smaller than the number you can see?

Put some beads on a lace to match this one of mine . . .

Now can you use that to help you work out how many I've got hidden?

Can you find a way of recording your work using pictures?

Using numbers?

Keeping going

◆ Various materials can be used in this activity — which is basically about partitioning sets. Try sealed plastic bags with a number of small toy animals inside (give them plenty of space so that some can be hidden under a hand); or use sticks of linking cubes which can be broken into two pieces and one piece hidden.

◆ Ask children to find all the ways of hiding beads on a given lace (for example, with 10 beads you can have 1 hidden and 9 showing, 2 hidden and 8 showing . . .).

◆ Ask children to find all the ways of threading 3 beads on a lace in just two colours. What about 4 or 5 beads?

Can the children . . .

thread 1, 2, 3, 4 or 5 beads on a lace according to instructions?

count the number of beads on a lace, up to 5?

pre-level 1

thread up to 10 beads on a lace according to instructions?

count the number of beads on a lace, up to at least 10?

use modelling (on fingers, or with another similar lace of beads) to work out how many beads are hidden, on a lace with up to 10 beads?

use 'counting on' to find how many beads are hidden?

record their work using pictures?

level 1

count beads in twos or tens, up to at least 100?

know how many beads are hidden, on a lace with up to 20 beads?

use modelling (on fingers, another similar lace of beads, or a number line) to work out how many beads are hidden, on a lace with up to 50 beads?

record their work using numbers?

level 2

on a lace threaded with equal sets of beads (totalling 25 or less), say how many sets are hidden? And how many beads?

on a lace threaded with beads in sets of five (totalling 50 or less), say how many sets are hidden? And how many beads?

on a lace threaded with beads in sets of ten (totalling 100 or less), say how many sets are hidden? And how many beads?

record their work using numbers?

level 3

MAKING NUMBERS

Children will experience
- reading two- and three-digit numbers
- recalling number facts
- thinking about the four operations
- being systematic

Equipment
- number cards 0-9
- cards showing the four operations

+	–	X	÷

- pencil and paper

Getting started

Give children three single-digit numbers and get them to write them down. Ask them to find all the ways they can of making other numbers from the three they have. (This might include adding, subtracting, multiplying — and possibly dividing — putting digits together to make two- and three-digit numbers and combinations of all these.)

Children who easily find 'all the answers' can try the same thing with another three digits, or attempt four digits.

As this activity is partly designed for you to assess children's recall of number facts and their ability to work out number problems, calculators should not be allowed.

Questions to ask the children

You've added those two numbers. Are there any more additions you could do?

How do you know you have them all?

You've put the 1 and 2 together. Can you read me that number?

You've done three addition sums. Can you think of any other addition sums you can make?

Any other kind of sums?

Why don't you two show each other your work. It might give both of you some more ideas.

Can you sort your answers? . . .

Can you think of any more you could do like those?

Keeping going

- ◆ Children can work in pairs. Each child chooses three numbers for the other to work on, then at the end checks what they have done.

- ◆ Children can find another three numbers by picking three cards at random from a pack of 0-9 cards.

- ◆ Children can choose for themselves what numbers to work on next.

- ◆ Some children might want to work with numbers over 9.

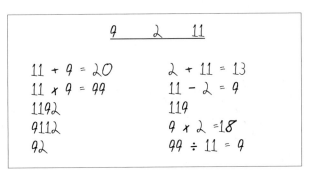

Can the children . . .

say the names of their three numbers (in the range 1-5)?

copy their three numbers (in the range 1-5)?

pre-level 1

say the names of any numbers in the range 0-10?

find a way of adding pairs of numbers whose total is no more than 10?

find a way of subtracting pairs of numbers in the range 0-10?

level 1

make and say the names of two-digit numbers?

recall addition pairs with numbers whose total is no more than 10?

find the difference between pairs of single-digit numbers?

level 2

make and say the names of three-digit numbers?

recall addition pairs with numbers whose total is no more than 20?

find the difference between a two-digit and a single-digit number?

find a way of multiplying any pair of single-digit numbers?

recall multiplication pairs in the 2, 5 and 10 multiplication tables?

be systematic in finding all the possibilities?

level 3

Checking, Estimating and Approximating

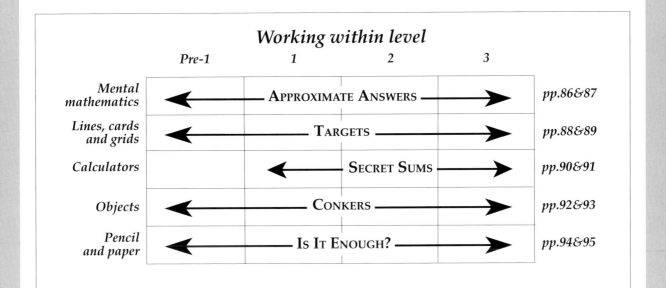

	Pre-1	1	2	3	
	Working within level				
Mental mathematics	←	APPROXIMATE ANSWERS		→	*pp.86&87*
Lines, cards and grids	←	TARGETS		→	*pp.88&89*
Calculators		←	SECRET SUMS	→	*pp.90&91*
Objects	←	CONKERS		→	*pp.92&93*
Pencil and paper	←	IS IT ENOUGH?		→	*pp.94&95*

APPROXIMATE ANSWERS

Children will experience

◆ making rough mental calculations
◆ developing mental methods

Equipment

◆ calculators
◆ number lines
◆ pencil and paper

Getting started

Introduce this activity to a group or to the whole class. Write down a sum and ask the children to work out an approximate answer in their head and write it down, emphasising that accurate answers are not necessary. Try to use sums where children do not know, and cannot easily work out, the answer. This will encourage them to use approximation. They can then use their calculators to find out the actual answer.

You may want to give children targets such as 'try and make sure your answer has the right number of digits in it' or 'try to reach an answer within 10 (or 20, 50, 100 . . .) of the actual answer'.

Later on, children can work in pairs. One can invent the sum and the other work out the approximate answer. (They will need to keep swapping roles, so that both have turns at mental calculation.)

Questions to ask the children

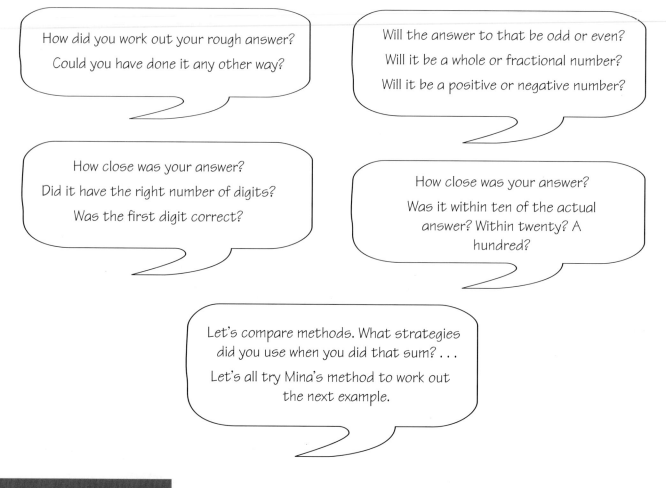

How did you work out your rough answer?
Could you have done it any other way?

Will the answer to that be odd or even?
Will it be a whole or fractional number?
Will it be a positive or negative number?

How close was your answer?
Did it have the right number of digits?
Was the first digit correct?

How close was your answer?
Was it within ten of the actual answer? Within twenty? A hundred?

Let's compare methods. What strategies did you use when you did that sum? . . .
Let's all try Mina's method to work out the next example.

Keeping going

◆ Whenever a real opportunity arises for rough calculations it can be used instead of this teaching session. In a real-life situation it is easier to know what degree of accuracy is appropriate. Such situations might be, for instance, buying enough fruit juice or making enough sandwiches for a party, or working out how much time is needed for everyone to show their dance in assembly.

◆ Children can work in groups, one writing a sum and everyone working out an approximate answer. Children can then share their methods with each other and you — a valuable way of learning about alternative mental methods.

Can the children . . .

give a rough estimate of how many biscuits are needed for a small group of children? *pre-level 1*	estimate how many children are in the home corner or book corner? *level 1*
mentally, find approximate answers to addition and subtraction sums using numbers under 30? mentally, find approximate answers to multiplication and division sums using numbers under 30? *level 2*	mentally, find approximate answers to addition and subtraction sums using numbers under 500? mentally, find approximate answers to multiplication and division sums using numbers under 100? *level 3*

TARGETS

Children will experience

◆ estimating the differences between pairs of numbers

◆ checking these differences on a number line

Equipment

◆ number cards 0-10 or 0-100

◆ number line 0-10 or 0-100

◆ number line 10 to –10

◆ fraction number line

◆ decimal number line

◆ 'money' number line

Getting started

Children work in a group of three or four. One child should shuffle the cards and turn over the top one. That is the target number and should be marked on the number line. Now each child takes one card from the rest of the pack. They show their cards to each other and estimate whose number is closest to the target. Each number is then checked on the number line.

Later children can try to work without reference to the line.

You could ask children to record their estimates and checks on a chart.

guess	check

Questions to ask the children

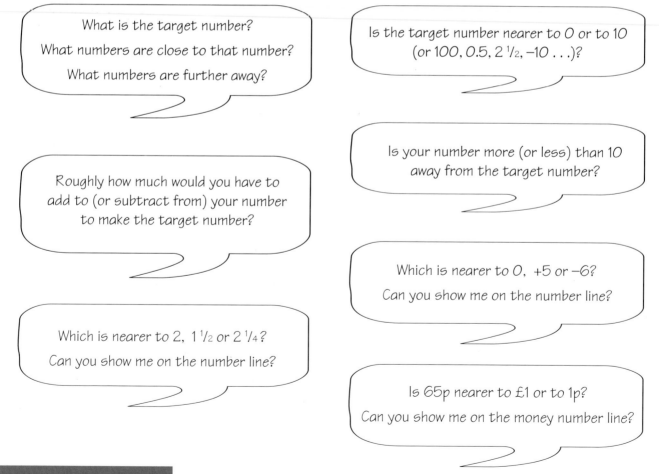

What is the target number?
What numbers are close to that number?
What numbers are further away?

Is the target number nearer to 0 or to 10 (or 100, 0.5, 2 ½, –10 . . .)?

Roughly how much would you have to add to (or subtract from) your number to make the target number?

Is your number more (or less) than 10 away from the target number?

Which is nearer to 0, +5 or –6?
Can you show me on the number line?

Which is nearer to 2, 1 ½ or 2 ¼?
Can you show me on the number line?

Is 65p nearer to £1 or to 1p?
Can you show me on the money number line?

Keeping going

◆ Children can work in pairs. They start with the number line turned face down. They pick two cards, estimate which will be closer to the target, and write down their guess. Then they check on the line.

◆ *Rounding up and down*
Children round the target number and the numbers on their cards up or down to the nearest 10 before estimating and working out who is closest to the target.

◆ Use cards with random numbers up to 1000 and a 0-1000 number line marked in tens. Children write on the line approximately where their numbers are.

◆ Use cards with random numbers up to 1000 and a 0-1000 number line marked in tens. Children round up and down to nearest ten. Later they can round up and down to the nearest hundred.

Can the children . . .

look at a 0-5 number line and say what numbers lie next to any other number?

pre-level 1

find their number and the target number on a 0-10 number line?

make sensible estimates, using visual clues, about whose number is closest to the target?

find which of two numbers is closest to the target number on a 0-10 number line by counting steps?

say whether their number or the target number is closer to 0 or 10?

level 1

find their number and the target number on a 0-100 number line?

make sensible estimates, using visual clues, about whose number is closest to the target?

find which of two numbers is closer to the target number on a 0-100 number line?

level 2

make sensible estimates about whose number is closest to the target using whole numbers 0-1000?
using whole numbers, halves and quarters?
using decimal numbers to one decimal place?
using positive and negative numbers?

round numbers up or down to the nearest 10 or 100?

make estimates using money and familiar measures?

level 3

SECRET SUMS

Children will experience

◆ thinking about the effects of the four operations on various numbers
◆ doing rough mental calculations
◆ checking mental calculations using the calculator

Equipment

◆ calculators
◆ pencil and paper

Getting started

Introduce this activity to a group of four to six children, working in pairs. Write down a sum in secret (for example, '12 – 2 = '), and tell the children the first number of the sum only (in this case 12). They should key this number in to their calculators and then close their eyes. You complete the operation on each calculator (pressing − 2 =). They then look at the result and try to work out what operation you did.

Later, children can work in pairs, taking turns to write the secret sum.

Questions to ask the children

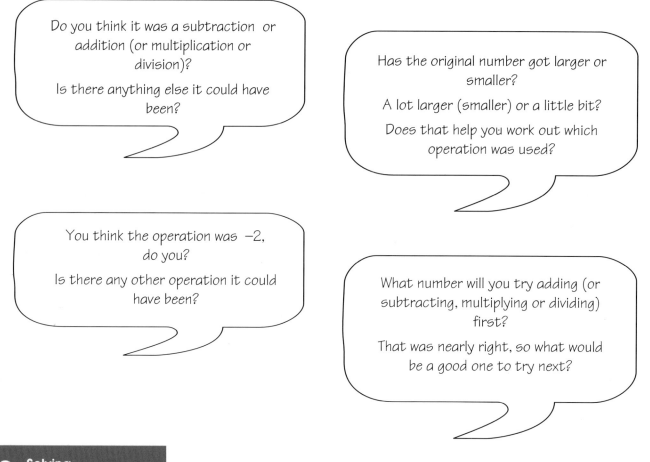

Do you think it was a subtraction or addition (or multiplication or division)?

Is there anything else it could have been?

Has the original number got larger or smaller?

A lot larger (smaller) or a little bit?

Does that help you work out which operation was used?

You think the operation was −2, do you?

Is there any other operation it could have been?

What number will you try adding (or subtracting, multiplying or dividing) first?

That was nearly right, so what would be a good one to try next?

Keeping going

◆ The child who wrote the secret sum can hold the other child's finger and use it to press the 'secret' keys. This gives their partner an inkling, but not a clear idea, of what keys were pressed.

◆ Younger or less confident children can simply try to find the operation used without worrying about the second number.

◆ Use the constant function to keep doing the same operation to any number inputted by the child. They have to use the information about what numbers they have put in, and how these are transformed, to work out the secret operation.

Can the children . . .

<table>
<tr>
<td>

not appropriate

pre-level 1
</td>
<td>

say which operation button was used when any single-digit number has been subtracted from (or added to) another single-digit number?

make a sensible guess as to the second number in the sum?

level 1
</td>
</tr>
<tr>
<td>

say which operation was used when any number between 0 and 20 has been subtracted from (or added to) another such number?

say which operation was used when any two single-digit numbers have been multiplied together?

say which operation was used when a number between 1 and 100 has been divided by a single-digit number?

make a sensible guess as to the second number in the sum?

level 2
</td>
<td>

say which operation was used when any number between 0 and 100 has been subtracted from (or added to) another such number?

say which operation was used when two numbers between 1 and 100 have been multiplied together?

say which operation was used when a number between 1 and 100 has been divided by a single-digit number — even if the answer contains a decimal fraction?

make a sensible guess as to the second number in the sum?   *level 3*
</td>
</tr>
</table>

CONKERS

Children will experience
◆ estimating the number of objects
◆ looking again to refine estimates
◆ comparing estimates with an actual count

Equipment
◆ conkers/bottletops/corks/buttons
◆ number line (0-10 or 0-30 or 0-100)
◆ linking cubes
◆ base ten blocks

Getting started

Children should work in a small group with you. Show them a handful of conkers then, before anyone has time to count, cover them with a cloth. It is important to emphasise that there isn't time to count — they can only guess.

Later children can count the conkers and use a number line to see how close their guesses were.

At levels 2 and 3 children can work with linking cubes in sticks of ten or base ten blocks.

Questions to ask the children

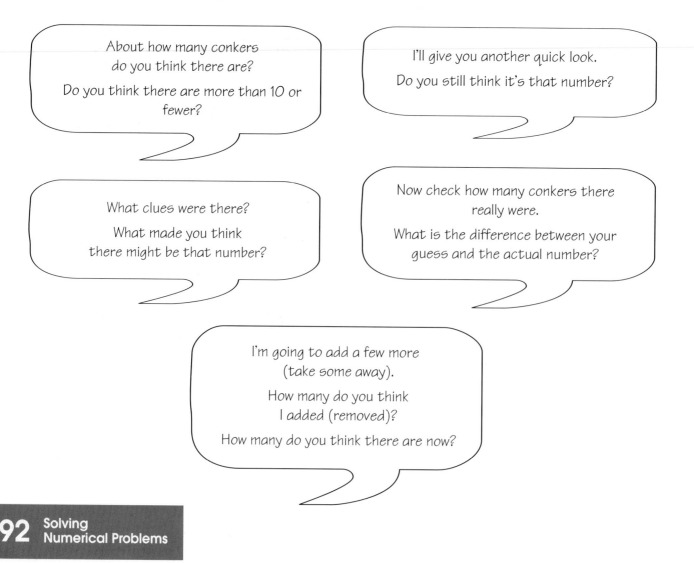

About how many conkers do you think there are?

Do you think there are more than 10 or fewer?

I'll give you another quick look.
Do you still think it's that number?

What clues were there?
What made you think there might be that number?

Now check how many conkers there really were.
What is the difference between your guess and the actual number?

I'm going to add a few more (take some away).
How many do you think I added (removed)?
How many do you think there are now?

Keeping going

◆ Children can use very small or very large objects (paper clips, sunflower seeds, apples, footballs . . .) and appropriately small or large things to cover them with (upside-down teacup, blanket . . .).

◆ Children can use a mixture of objects of different sizes — for instance, small and large buttons all jumbled together.

◆ Estimate other things — the number of pages in a book, books in the school, grains of rice in a pound (cooked and uncooked), leaves on a tree, trees in the world . . .

Can the children . . .

make sensible estimates when there are five or fewer conkers?

use number names up to 5?

check the actual amount when there are five or fewer conkers?

pre-level 1

make sensible estimates when there are ten or fewer conkers?

check the actual amount when there are ten or fewer conkers?

use number names up to at least 10?

find their estimate and the actual number on a 0-10 number line?

use familiar patterns in the way the conkers are lying to help them estimate? (for example, o o is four)
o o

level 1

make sensible estimates when there are 100 or fewer objects?

use number names up to 100?

check the actual amount when there are up to 100 objects by grouping and counting in twos, fives or tens?

find their estimate and the actual number on a 0-100 number line?

find the difference between an estimate and the actual number on a 0-100 number line?

level 2

make sensible estimates when there are 1000 or fewer objects?

use number names up to 1000?

check the actual amount when there are up to 1000 objects by grouping and counting in tens and hundreds?

find the difference between an estimate and the actual number using a method of their choice?

level 3

Is It Enough?

Children will experience

◆ approximate mental addition
◆ estimating quantities

Equipment

◆ ordinary dice (with dots)
◆ blank dice for higher numbers
◆ pencil and paper
◆ egg boxes (for both 6 and 12 eggs)
◆ cubes
◆ number lines
◆ calculators

Getting started

Children can work in a group of three or four. Give them a target range (such as
10 to 15, 20 to 30 or 90 to 100). Each child tosses a dice and writes down the number they
get. (Young children can draw the number of dots.) As a group they then estimate whether,
if they add their numbers, they will have scored a number within their target range. (For
example, three children throw a 2, a 4 and a 6. Their total is 12, which is in their target range
of 10 to 15.)

Very young children will need to use concrete materials. They could collect cubes and
estimate whether they have enough to put one in each section of an egg box.

Questions to ask the children

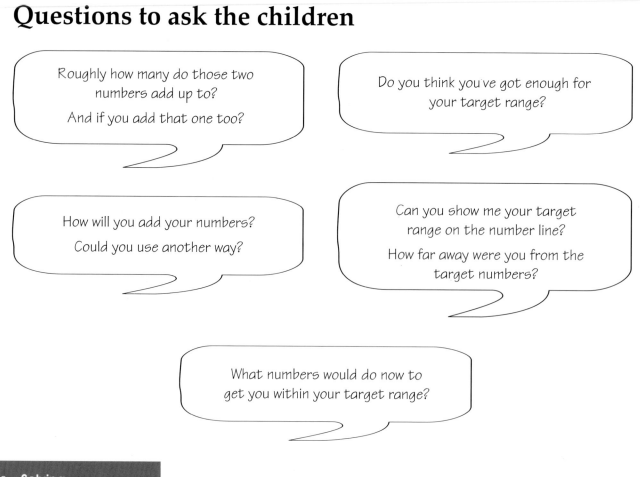

Roughly how many do those two
numbers add up to?

And if you add that one too?

Do you think you've got enough for
your target range?

How will you add your numbers?

Could you use another way?

Can you show me your target
range on the number line?

How far away were you from the
target numbers?

What numbers would do now to
get you within your target range?

Keeping going

◆ Young children can collect various things — conkers to fill a bun tray, stickers to make dots on a ladybird, matchsticks to make legs for a monster . . . The important thing is not to put the legs on the monster (or equivalent) until the dice-throws are complete, and then to *estimate* whether there are enough before doing it.

◆ Older children, aiming for higher targets, could use two dice for each throw, one showing tens numbers and one units. They can use calculators to check their estimates.

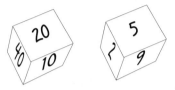

Can the children . . .

<table>
<tr>
<td>

make a sensible estimate about whether their cubes will fill the 6 spaces in a small eggbox?

pre-level 1
</td>
<td>

make a sensible estimate about whether their cubes will fill the 12 spaces in a large eggbox?

make a sensible estimate of the total number of dots they have drawn up to 20?

level 1
</td>
</tr>
<tr>
<td>

make a sensible estimate about what three single-digit numbers will total?

check the total of these three numbers?

find the difference between their estimate and the actual number?

level 2
</td>
<td>

make a sensible estimate about what three single- or two-digit numbers will total?

check this total?

find the difference between their estimate and the actual number?

level 3
</td>
</tr>
</table>

Solving Numerical Problems

Applying Operations

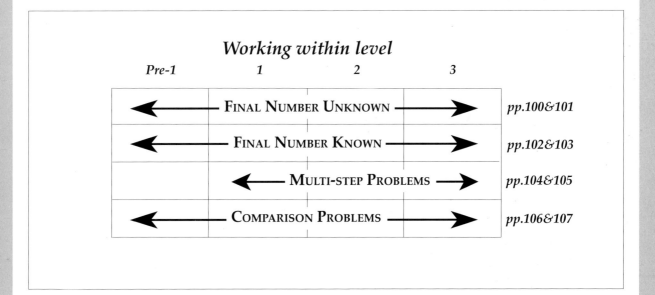

Working within level			
Pre-1	*1*	*2*	*3*
← FINAL NUMBER UNKNOWN →				*pp.100&101*
← FINAL NUMBER KNOWN →				*pp.102&103*
← MULTI-STEP PROBLEMS →				*pp.104&105*
← COMPARISON PROBLEMS →				*pp.106&107*

97

Applying Operations: Introduction

Activities in this section

This section does not follow the same pattern as the previous sections, which included one activity for each of the five tools: mental mathematics; lines, cards and grids; calculators; objects; and pencil and paper.

In this section there are four activities, in the form of word problems. None of these is particularly suited to any one tool. Each problem could be tackled using any of the five tools, and indeed we suggest that children are encouraged to experiment with using more than one of the tools to work on a problem, in order to get a different angle on it and to help them make links between different methods of problem solving.

The four activities included in this section have been chosen to provide a range of types and to indicate the kind of problem that can be developed from common classroom topics and events.

The importance of word problems

Often children learn to respond to the operation signs when they see them written, but when faced with a word problem do not know whether to add, subtract or what! Sometimes the words can mislead children. For instance, one child was asked to solve the following problem: 'Jan gives 10 plums to each of her two friends. How many is that altogether?' She heard the word 'altogether' and thought 'that means add', so added the two friends to the ten plums and came up with the answer twelve.

In order that children learn to deal with word problems appropriately they need experience of working with them from early on, using all of the five tools, but especially modelling with number lines, objects and drawings, and finding their own ways of recording.

Written work

When children are asked to record their work on the problems in this section — or others like them — you will probably find that they use all sorts of different methods of recording. At the early levels children will not use the conventional operation signs (+ − x and ÷). Later, when they are more familiar with these signs, you can encourage them to use them. But even then you may find that they use different operations from what you expect. For instance, suppose children have worked on this problem: 'Metin baked some currant buns. We ate 3 and there were 9 left. How many did he bake?'. You may expect children to see this as a subtraction sum, and some may: ? − 3 = 9. But others may choose to regard it as an addition: 3 + 9 = ?.

Providing a range of problems

All number operations that primary age children do can be reduced to addition, subtraction, multiplication and division. However the word problems they deal with cannot be categorised so easily. As we saw, the problem just mentioned, concerning Metin and his buns, can be viewed as either an addition or a subtraction — real life just doesn't come in neat packages labelled 'addition', 'subtraction', 'multiplication' and 'division'.

It is important that the problems we give children are 'real' in this sense: problems where they have to work out for themselves what operations to use and how to apply them. To help you provide a range of problems we have suggested four different kinds in this section, each of which could involve any of the four operations. If you make sure that children work on problems of each type, you are likely to provide a fair balance overall.

The four types of problem

The final quantity is unknown (the traditional kind of problem is mostly of this type)

Metin baked 12 currant buns and 10 cherry buns. How many did he bake altogether?

or

Metin baked some buns in 12-bun tins. He used two full tins. How many buns did he bake?

or

Jan shared 20 plums between her four friends. How many did each person get?

The final quantity is known but not all the steps on the way

Metin baked 20 currant buns. Someone went down in the night and ate some. The next morning he found there were only 15 left. How many were eaten?

or

Metin wants to bake 24 buns. Each tin will hold 12 buns, so how many tins does he need?

or

We had 15 leaves for the nature table. We had to sort out the leaves we thought were mostly brown. We decided that 12 leaves were. How many weren't?

Multi-step problems

I picked up 5 leaves to take to school and I found another 7 and another 3. How many leaves did I take to school altogether?

or

I collected 15 leaves for the nature table. My friends had no leaves, so I gave one 4 and the other 3 of mine. How many leaves did I take into school?

or

I have enough wheels for 3 cars and there will be 2 over. How many wheels do I have?

Problems which involve comparisons between two or more sets

My teacher asked me to work with a partner to look at each other's leaves. My partner had 25 leaves and I only had 17. How many more leaves did she have than me?

or

I've got 5 leaves, Mike has 3 and Sheila has 12. Who has most? How many more has Sheila got than Mike or me?

FINAL NUMBER UNKNOWN

Children will experience
- selecting appropriate mathematics
- selecting appropriate materials
- choosing a way of representing work
- communicating findings

Equipment
- children's minds
- number lines
- calculators
- objects such as counters, linking cubes or base ten blocks
- pencil and paper

Getting started

Ask the children to listen as you tell a simple number story where the final quantity is unknown — it might involve addition, subtraction, multiplication or division.

One teacher used the following story: 'We are going to buy some bulbs and compost to plant them in. I've got £6 here to spend on the bulbs and another £3 for the compost. How much money have I got altogether?'

Another teacher used the following: 'There are 30 children in the class and I want you to get into groups of 5. How many groups will that be?'

Some children may be able to find the answer mentally. Children could also solve the problem practically by modelling it in some way — perhaps with counters or on the number line.

Encourage them to find a way of recording their discoveries too, using pictures or numbers.

Questions to ask the children

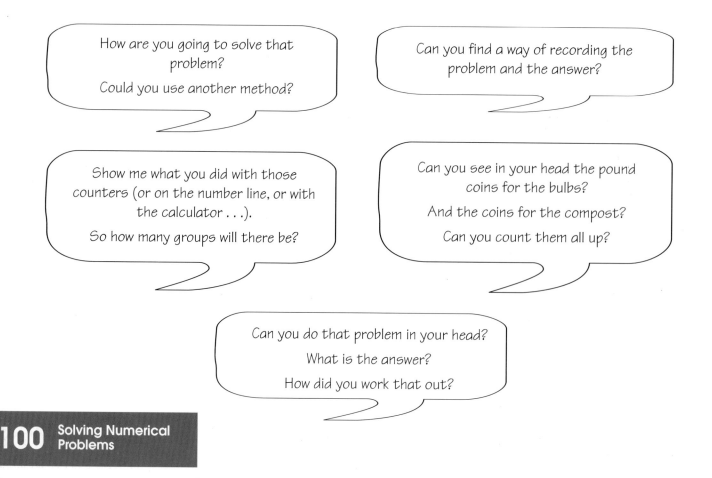

How are you going to solve that problem?

Could you use another method?

Can you find a way of recording the problem and the answer?

Show me what you did with those counters (or on the number line, or with the calculator . . .).

So how many groups will there be?

Can you see in your head the pound coins for the bulbs?

And the coins for the compost?

Can you count them all up?

Can you do that problem in your head?

What is the answer?

How did you work that out?

Keeping going

◆ Tell the children other number stories. Can they say what operation is involved — addition, subtraction, multiplication or division? Why can some stories be both addition and subtraction (or multiplication and division)?

◆ Tell the children other problems to do with familiar contexts.

◆ Children can pick two number cards at random and use them to make up as many different sums as they can.

◆ Work with a small group and ask the children to take turns to make up a number problem. The rest of the group work together to solve the problem. Encourage them to try different methods — drawing steps on a number line, working mentally, modelling with counters . . .

◆ Everyone in the class or group can make up one problem. Shuffle them up and deal them out, one to each child. Then children work in pairs to solve their two problems.

Can the children . . .

put two sets of objects together and count how many there are in the combined set — with numbers up to 5?

pre-level 1

use counters to represent a simple addition or subtraction problem with numbers up to at least 10?

draw a picture of a simple addition or subtraction situation and use that to help them work out the answer, for numbers up to at least 10?

decide how to use the number line to model a simple addition or subtraction problem involving numbers up to at least 10?

recognise when they have found the answer and say what it is?

level 1

decide on a method of solving a simple problem with numbers up to at least 20?

recognise when they have found the answer and say what it is?

write a number sentence of their choice to describe a situation, for numbers up to at least 20?

explain what the numbers in their number sentence represent?

level 2

use either of two different methods for solving a problem with numbers up to at least 100?

write a number sentence of their choice to describe a situation, for numbers up to at least 100?

recognise what operation or operations will be needed to solve a given problem?

explain what the numbers in their number sentence represent?

level 3

FINAL NUMBER KNOWN

Children will experience
◆ selecting appropriate mathematics
◆ selecting appropriate materials
◆ choosing a way of representing work
◆ communicating findings

Equipment
◆ children's minds
◆ number lines
◆ calculators
◆ objects such as counters, linking cubes or base ten blocks
◆ pencil and paper

Getting started

Ask the children to listen as you tell a story based on a topic of current interest. The story should be one where the final quantity is known but one of the other quantities is unknown.

One teacher adapted this story from a popular library book: 'A girl called Jo baked some tarts. Her little dog stole 3 of them during the night. In the morning she saw there were only 3 left.' Ask the children to tell you how many tarts Jo had baked.

Make up some similar stories in which the final quantity is known, and ask the children to illustrate one of these stories. Some children should be able to write a 'sum' to go with the story. (The situation is not one where just one sum describes it. Children may come up with, for instance, an addition — 'There were 3 tarts stolen and 3 tarts still there which makes 6.' Or they may invent a subtraction — 'There were 6 tarts and the dog stole 3 which leaves 3.' Or they may find yet another solution.)

Questions to ask the children

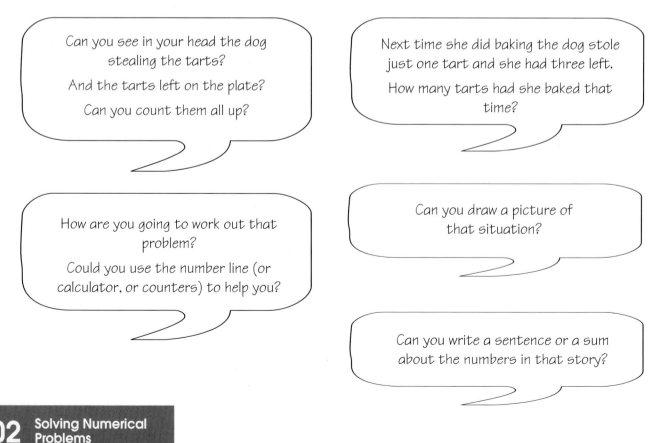

Can you see in your head the dog stealing the tarts?

And the tarts left on the plate?

Can you count them all up?

Next time she did baking the dog stole just one tart and she had three left.

How many tarts had she baked that time?

How are you going to work out that problem?

Could you use the number line (or calculator, or counters) to help you?

Can you draw a picture of that situation?

Can you write a sentence or a sum about the numbers in that story?

Keeping going

◆ Tell the children more stories based on Jo and the tarts. For example, 'Jo baked 10 tarts and in the night the dog stole some. Next morning there were only 4 left. How many had the dog taken?'

Or, 'Jo baked 10 tarts. She used two kinds of jam. Five were gooseberry jam and the rest were raspberry. How many were raspberry?' This leads on to the exploration of other ways of partitioning ten — such as 1 gooseberry and 9 raspberry tarts.

◆ Give children the following problem: 'The answer is 10, what was the question?'

Can the children . . .

partition a set of objects and count how many objects there are in each sub-set — with numbers up to 5?
pre-level 1

use counters to represent a simple addition or subtraction problem with numbers up to at least 10?
draw a picture of a simple addition or subtraction situation and use that to help them work out the answer, for numbers up to at least 10?
decide how to use the number line to model a simple addition or subtraction problem involving numbers up to at least 10?
recognise when they have found the answer and say what it is?
level 1

decide on a method of solving a simple problem with numbers up to at least 20?
recognise when they have found the answer and say what it is?
write a number sentence of their choice to describe a situation, for numbers up to at least 20?
explain what the numbers in their number sentence represent?
level 2

use either of two different methods for solving a problem with numbers up to at least 100?
write a number sentence of their choice to describe a situation, for numbers up to at least 100?
recognise what operation or operations will be needed to solve a given problem?
explain what the numbers in their number sentence represent?
level 3

MULTI-STEP STORIES

Children will experience
◆ selecting appropriate mathematics
◆ selecting appropriate materials
◆ choosing a way of representing work
◆ communicating findings

Equipment
◆ children's minds
◆ number lines
◆ calculators
◆ objects such as counters, linking cubes or base ten blocks
◆ pencil and paper

Getting started

Ask the children to listen as you tell a multi-step number story. One teacher used the following story, based on some work the class had been doing on leaves: 'Sam has been collecting different kinds of leaf. On Monday he found five leaves. On Tuesday he found another three. Then he found one leaf on Wednesday. How many leaves has Sam collected altogether this week?'

Multi-step addition and subtraction problems are particularly suitable for solving on a calculator. Children could also model this problem with counters or on the number line. Encourage them to find a way of recording their discoveries too, using pictures or numbers.

(Children who are not ready for modelling a situation such as this on the line may need more experience doing simple games and activities about taking steps on the line. You could also introduce them to simpler modelling situations, where just one is added each time.)

Questions to ask the children

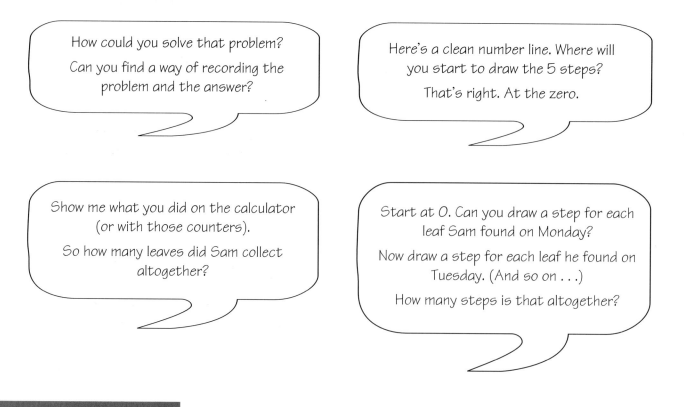

How could you solve that problem?

Can you find a way of recording the problem and the answer?

Here's a clean number line. Where will you start to draw the 5 steps?

That's right. At the zero.

Show me what you did on the calculator (or with those counters).

So how many leaves did Sam collect altogether?

Start at 0. Can you draw a step for each leaf Sam found on Monday?

Now draw a step for each leaf he found on Tuesday. (And so on . . .)

How many steps is that altogether?

Keeping going

◆ Tell the children multi-step stories involving subtraction as well as addition. Earning and spending money is a good topic to use for problems of this nature.

◆ Ask the children to make up their own multi-step stories — in writing or on audiotape. They could work in pairs with each child making up a story for their partner to tackle.

◆ Make number story cards on a theme. For example, cards about a stable full of horses might include: 'Two horses came to stay' 'One horse left' 'Five foals were born'. The children start with a number such as 20 (horses in this case), then pick cards one at a time, keeping track of the running total of animals in whatever way they like.

Ask the children what will happen if they pick the same cards in a different order. Will they still get the same end result?

Can the children . . .

<table>
<tr><td>

not appropriate

pre-level 1
</td><td>

use counters to represent a simple addition or subtraction problem with numbers up to at least 10?

draw a picture of a simple addition or subtraction situation and use that to help them work out the answer, for numbers up to at least 10?

decide how to use the number line to model a simple addition or subtraction problem involving numbers up to at least 10?

recognise when they have found the answer and say what it is?

level 1
</td></tr>
<tr><td>

decide on a method of solving a multi-step problem with numbers up to at least 20?

recognise when they have found the answer and say what it is?

write a number sentence of their choice to describe a multi-step problem, for numbers up to at least 20?

explain what the numbers in their number sentence represent?

level 2
</td><td>

use either of two different methods for solving a problem with numbers up to at least 100?

recognise what operation or operations will be needed to solve a given problem?

write a number sentence of their choice to describe a situation, for numbers up to at least 100?

explain what the numbers in their number sentence represent?

level 3
</td></tr>
</table>

COMPARISON STORIES

Children will experience
◆ selecting appropriate mathematics
◆ selecting appropriate materials
◆ choosing a way of representing work
◆ communicating findings

Equipment
◆ children's minds
◆ number lines
◆ calculators
◆ objects such as counters, linking cubes or base ten blocks
◆ pencil and paper

Getting started

Ask the children to listen as you tell a comparing number story. One teacher used the following problem, based on some work the class had been doing on greetings cards: 'Fiona has sorted her collection of cards and stuck them in her book. She has got 5 birthday cards, 12 postcards, 2 Mother's Day cards and an Easter card. Which are there most of? . . . How many more postcards are there than birthday cards? . . . Than Easter cards?'

If the cards (or other objects) are available for moving about, children can do direct comparisons. Otherwise they will need to work mentally, use a calculator, or model the problem in some way.

Encourage them to find a way of recording their discoveries too, using pictures or numbers.

Questions to ask the children

How could you solve that problem?
How will you record the problem and the answer?

You've ringed the numbers of cards on the number line.
How can you use that to work out how many more postcards there are than birthday cards?

How could you solve that problem?
Might you be able to do it another way?

Show me what you did with those counters . . .
So how many more postcards are there than birthday cards?

Keeping going

◆ Tell the children more comparison stories. Can they solve each one using a different method?

◆ Pairs of children can play *Collect the Difference*. Each child picks a number card at random from a pack. The children work out the difference between the two numbers. That is their score for this turn. They keep picking cards, finding the difference and adding this to their score until they have reached 50 (or 100).

◆ Three children each pick a number card at random from a pack. They work out all the possible differences between their three numbers. Which is the greatest difference and which is the smallest?

Can the children . . .

use direct comparison to say which of two sets is greater?

pre-level 1

use counters to represent a simple comparing problem with numbers up to at least 10?

draw a picture of a simple comparing situation and use that to help them work out the answer, for numbers up to at least 10?

decide how to use the number line to model a simple comparing problem involving numbers up to at least 10?

recognise when they have found the answer and say what it is?

level 1

decide on a method of solving a simple problem with numbers up to at least 20?

recognise when they have found the answer and say what it is?

write a number sentence of their choice to describe a situation, for numbers up to at least 20?

explain what the numbers in their number sentence represent?

level 2

use either of two different methods for solving a problem with numbers up to at least 100?

write a number sentence of their choice to describe a situation, for numbers up to at least 100?

recognise what operation or operations will be needed to solve a given problem?

explain what the numbers in their number sentence represent?

level 3

Resources

Number Cards

Blank cards and 0-100 cards are available from AMS Educational. They are the same size and material as standard playing cards.

AMS Educational, Woodside Trading Estate, Low Lane, Horsforth, Leeds LS18 5NY
Tel 01532 580309 Fax 01532 580133

Number Lines

BEAM sells 1m long number lines made of brightly coloured card, laminated to protect them and provided with a surface which children can write on with felt-tipped pens and then wipe clean. The 0-30 lines have intervals of roughly 25mm and an unnumbered line with 30 intervals on the reverse. The 0-100 lines have intervals of just under 10mm and an unnumbered line with 100 intervals on the reverse.

BEAM, Barnsbury Complex, Offord Road, London N1 1QH
Tel 0171-457 5535 Fax 0171-457 5906

Portable and wall number lines, originally produced by the ILEA Learning Resources Branch, are now available from AMS Educational. The portable lines are 100 cm long, made from tough plastic, and can be written on with a felt-tipped pen, then wiped clean. The plastic wall lines are 3m long and can also be written on with a felt-tipped pen, then wiped clean.

AMS Educational, Woodside Trading Estate, Low Lane, Horsforth, Leeds LS18 5NY
Tel 01532 580309 Fax 01532 580133

Slimwam 2

This is a collection of six computer programs suitable for children. Two of them, 'Monty' and 'Counter', are useful as extensions to activities in this book. Slimwam 2 is available for BBC, Archimedes and Nimbus.

Association of Teachers of Mathematics, 7 Shaftesbury Street, Derby DE23 8YB
Tel 01332 346599 Fax 01332 204357

Number Games

These 26 strategic number games for the computer were devised by Anita Straker. They encourage a range of skills including mental mathematics, strategic and logical thinking and the making and testing of simple hypotheses. The games include 'Boxes' and 'Trains' which are useful as extensions to activities in this book. This program is available only for the RM Nimbus.

LETSS, The Lodge, Crownwoods, Riefield Road, Eltham, London SE9 0AQ
Tel 0181-850 0100 Fax 0181-850 0400

Acknowledgments

We would like to thank the following Tower Hamlets teachers who initiated this book, and their schools who supported them:

Sîan Acreman and Thomas Buxton Junior School

Jenny Barlex and St Paul's with St Luke's Primary School

Tamara Bibby and Bonner Primary School

Pat Bolton and St John the Baptist Junior School

Sheila Coleman and Old Ford Infant School

Diana Curtis and Stewart Headlam Primary School

Kirsten Dwyer and Halley Primary School

Arlene Fitzpatrick and Clara Grant Primary School

Susan Garner and Manorfield Primary School

Joan Gill and Thomas Buxton Infant School

Sandra Holmes and Guardian Angels Primary School

Sarah Howes and Bigland Green Primary School

Jonathan Humphreys and Sir William Burrough Primary School

Moyra Lajmir and Old Church Nursery School

Mark Mee and Marner Primary School

Ann Mosol and St Mary and St Michael Junior School

Christine Mansbridge and Susan Lawrence Infant School

Bronagh Nugent and English Martyrs Primary School

Sandra Roberts and Shapla Primary School

Gerry Slamon and Wellington Primary School

Sue Walsh and Ben Jonson Primary School

Caroline Whittle and Columbia Primary School

Gary Witherford and Blue Gate Fields Junior School

We would like to thank the following teachers and schools for trialling the activities in this book, and suggesting helpful changes:

In Islington

Mel Ahmet and Thornhill Primary School

Shirley Beswick and Canonbury Infant School

Naomi Brest and William Tyndale Primary School

Catherine Clark and Prior Weston Primary School

Peter Clarke and Blessed Sacrament Primary School

Kim Connor and St John Evangelist Primary School

Sarah Duckham and St Mary's CE Primary School

Sophie Norburn and Penton Primary School

John Spooner and Rotherfield Junior School

Elsewhere

Gareth Williams, Downhills Junior School, Haringey

Carden Junior School, Chiddingly School, and the Brighton BEAM group

BEAM Director   Sheila Ebbutt

BEAM Editor and Designer   Fran Mosley

BEAM Project devised by   Lynda Maple and Anita Straker

About BEAM

BEAM is a curriculum development project for primary mathematics. We publish a range of materials and run an in-service programme for teachers in primary, nursery and special schools. Our aims are to:

- develop teachers' understanding of mathematics
- help them find a way of teaching which fits with the way children learn mathematics
- provide support for the implementation of the national curriculum for mathematics

For further information on BEAM publications or courses please get in touch with Sheila Ebbutt at:

BEAM, Barnsbury Complex, Offord Road, London N1 1QH
Tel 0171-457 5535 Fax 0171-457 5906